UNESCO and the Fate of 1

Post 45 Loren Glass and Kate Marshall, Editors
Post•45 Group, Editorial Committee

UNESCO and the Fate of the Literary

Sarah Brouillette

Stanford University Press

Stanford, California

STANFORD UNIVERSITY PRESS

Stanford, California

© 2019 by the Board of Trustees of the Leland Stanford Junior University.
All rights reserved.

No part of this book may be reproduced or transmitted in any form or by any means, electronic or mechanical, including photocopying and recording, or in any information storage or retrieval system without the prior written permission of Stanford University Press.

Printed in the United States of America on acid-free, archival-quality paper

Library of Congress Cataloging-in-Publication Data
Names: Brouillette, Sarah.
Title: UNESCO and the fate of the literary / Sarah Brouillette.
Description: Stanford, California : Stanford University Press, 2019. |
Series: Post•45 | Includes bibliographical references and index.
Identifiers: LCCN 2018057613 (print) | LCCN 2018060097 (ebook) |
ISBN 9781503609952 (cloth: alk. paper) | ISBN 9781503610316 (pbk. : alk. paper) |
ISBN 9781503610323 (ebook)
Subjects: LCSH: Literature—Philosophy—History. | Unesco—History. |
Books and reading—International cooperation—History. | Book industries and trade—International cooperation—History. | Cultural policy—Economic aspects—History.
Classification: LCC PN45 (ebook) | LCC PN45 .B748 2019 (print) | DDC 801—DC23
LC record available at https://lccn.loc.gov/2018057613

Cover design: Rob Ehle

Typeset by Kevin Barrett Kane in 10/15 Minion Pro

Contents

Acknowledgments   vii

Introduction   1

1   **UNESCO's Collection of Representative Works**   21

2   **America's Postwar Hegemony**   37

3   **Cultural Policy and the Perils of Development**   55

4   **Book Hunger**   77

5   **Policy Making for the Creative Industries Today**   99

6   **Pirates and Pipe Dreams**   123

Conclusion   139

Notes   149

Bibliography   157

Index   165

Acknowledgments

Research for this book was supported by the Social Sciences and Humanities Research Council of Canada and by grants and fellowships provided by Carleton University. At Carleton University I also have the good fortune to be supported by my excellent colleagues in the Department of English.

An earlier form of chapter 4 appeared as "UNESCO and the Book in the Developing World" in *Representations* 127.1 (2014): 33–54. Parts of chapter 5, framed differently, appeared in *Amodern* in December 2015. Parts of chapter 6, also framed differently, appeared in *Blind Field* in August 2017.

I have always relied heavily on my research assistants. Recently, I have been lucky to work with Dessa Bayrock, Adam Benn, John Coleman, and Shaun Stevenson. David Thomas is always there. Allie Watson worked especially hard on the final stages. My friends, thank you.

I am grateful to other scholars who have informed and engaged with material in this book. They include Timothy Aubry, Mark Banks, Jasper Bernes, Joshua Clover, Amy De'Ath, Arne DeBoever, Matt Hart, Tim Kreiner, Annie McClanahan, Mathias Nilges, Julianna Spahr, Emilio Sauri, and Michael Szalay.

In daily life, Travis DeCook supports me more than anyone else. He is a humble and courageous parent and scholar. I learn from his example, but not as much as I should.

At present I do not have the words to thank Grant Vogl. Fortunately, I have no doubt that there will be many more occasions.

Finally, this book is dedicated to a sweet child and my constant companion, Ben DeCook—a boundless creative spirit, totally ungovernable.

UNESCO and the Fate of the Literary

Introduction

UNESCO, or the United Nations Educational, Scientific and Cultural Organization, is the most important global institution for cultural policy formation. Although it has often supported literary culture, its sheer institutional complexity and dizzying myriad of programs have no doubt deterred scholars of literature from engaging much with it. UNESCO's approaches to literature have always been fundamentally tied to the broad and complex conflicts at work within the organization, which are themselves inextricable from global economic and political conditions. UNESCO is both a product and an engine of liberal social policy. Something similar can be said of its relation to postwar literary culture, though with the proviso that the place of literature within liberal policy making has changed considerably over the course of the postwar period. That transformation is my concern here.

In its earliest years, UNESCO conscripted literature into the project of supporting liberal cosmopolitanism. It viewed the translation of classic literature as a contribution to the work of forging the strong cross-border bonds that were thought at the time to be integral to world peace. Subsequently, in the decolonizing 1960s and 1970s, illiteracy and a lack of access to literary books were lamented as a "book hunger" in the developing world, and the idea of reading as an unquestionably humanizing universal value was used to argue, though unsuccessfully, for a more balanced communications industry and copyright regime. Finally, in recent years, literature has been brought into the branding of cities and nations as a part of the heritage industry and as a tourism product associated with programming in the UNESCO Creative Cities Network. Now, UNESCO largely treats high literature as a commercially self-sustaining leisure product for wealthy, aging publics and unlikely to do much for people living in impoverished conditions.

The original role imagined for literature as helping to forge an enlightened global polity has not been entirely abandoned by policy makers. It is, however, no longer a programming priority. The idea that literature offers unique evidence of fundamental human dignity and particularity is still powerful, as is literature's association with values of care and attention. UNESCO now simply tends to treat this association as the habit of an elite niche. Serving readers "hungry for books" in underdeveloped markets is no longer treated as a viable goal for policy, and fundamental policy reform that might address uneven relations within global intellectual property creation is very much off the table. UNESCO's literary programming is highly suggestive in this context. A trajectory that may appear to be one of triumphant success—literary tourism and festival programming can be quite lucrative for some people—is also, in a different light, a story of decline.

* * *

Tracing the history of UNESCO's support for literature—from liberalism through decolonizing left-liberalism to neoliberalism, if you like—is one way of grounding the critical discourse of world literature in the political economy of global literary institutions and markets. It is a way of analyzing the social forms in which we are ourselves participants and of avoiding approaches to the subject that are designed to console rather than politicize, within the setting of unfolding global crises of which literature's changed status is simply one minor sign. An economically focused version of cultural materialism, committed to examining the conditions of production of the literary cultural milieu, will be useful for this analysis. Yet we will venture significantly beyond the common delimitation of such inquiry to what Pierre Bourdieu describes as the field of cultural production, rooting our analysis of culture instead in a reckoning with the foundational structures of our societies. Whereas Bourdieusian theorists have extensively detailed the relations internal to a restricted literary field, considering how social class informs one's place in the cultural production system, this book emphasizes how cultural production emerges in relation to the real economy.

In emphasizing the real economy as a foundational context for the emergence and meaning of culture, I draw more from work on global economic turbulence and capitalist crises than from theories of the literary field.[1] These fields of study can, however, be brought together to allow us to study literature as a site of reproduction of people with certain dispositions—dispositions that complement, contest, or engage ambivalently with styles of governance that are themselves shaped by underlying economic realities. The literary field and the cultural policy-making milieu overlap in several respects. They share personnel and, often, ways of thinking. Literature has often served as equipment for cultural policy making. It helps to shape the mentalities of cultural policy makers, and those policy makers in turn develop ways to use literature as an aid to their own progressive governance. Developments in the global economy are a constitutive frame for their policy discussions, but cultural policy rarely greets those developments happily. Instead, a wary grimace is often common, as policy makers imagine how they can intervene in, guide, and reform economic systems to better meet human needs. Transformations in postwar literary culture can be seen in a new light through attention to this policy imaginary, placed in relation to the shifting states of the global economy and the dominant ideologies and cultural policy directives attached to them.

* * *

Despite their adherence to some form of Marxism, recent accounts of world literature have preferred to highlight works with congenial political tendencies rather than grounding their analysis in the sociology of high art and the shifting fortunes of literature's social effects. Their celebrations of a critical world-literary mode imply that literature reaches a substantial audience of uninitiated readers who need to learn what writers want to teach them. Research by the Warwick Research Collective (WReC) is a good example. They quite convincingly use the theory of combined and uneven development to explain formal developments in world literature. They suggest that world literature originating in semi-peripheral countries is particularly well positioned to counter capitalist modernity, as it features multiple narrative temporalities, disjunctive and dueling worldviews, and irrealisms. They claim that a "dissenting registration" of capitalist modernity, evident in these formal traits, is characteristic of the world-literary field.[2] Similarly, Pheng Cheah's *What Is a World?* argues that world literature at its best "attempts to remake the world against capitalist globalization," enabling "the opening of new worlds against the globalizing grain."[3]

We can be wholly on board with the opposition to capitalist globalization and yet still ask: To whom is literature's countering force relevant? To what audience of literary readers does it speak? Is it not also the case that the tropes of "against the grain" and "counter-modernity" are integral to the growth and expansion of world-literary industries and to the liberal cultural milieu of institutions like UNESCO? They are features of a general literary disposition that has helped to make UNESCO's policy work forceful and relevant. The idealization of literature's revelatory insights is a key part of literary socialization. It is fundamental to how institutions of world-literary production have sold themselves and justified their own relevance. In the case of UNESCO, the ideal of supporting the development of capacities to express local particularities has been key to all its work since the late 1960s. It has established its institutional legitimacy and the legitimacy of its cultural policy-making activities on the grounds of its promotion of unity amid diversity, particularity within universality. Support for local literary activity has been a part of this legitimation process.

Literary scholarship celebrating the radical potential of a critical anti-capitalist or counter-modernity message fails even to reach UNESCO's standard. For UNESCO has at least hosted and supported efforts to fix the unevenness of global communications infrastructures. It has given high-level platforms to people who recognize that this unevenness is rooted in the impoverishing colonial relations of expropriation and extraction that have left postcolonial states with little upon which to build "modern" or "advanced" communications industries. Scholarship on world literature, meanwhile, has almost wholly overlooked the fact that uneven development and capitalist "peripheralization" (Cheah 193) are more than tragic themes or occasions for formal experimentation within literature. They instead infect all literary activity, influencing who can write professionally and who has access to literary experiences that may or may not be affecting. Even as it takes the depredations of capitalism as one of its key targets, a developed high-literary culture able to sustain professional livelihoods is an affordance of relative wealth. Writers who grow up in places that have underdeveloped economies often leave, and their target audiences, editors, agents, and publishers are often elsewhere. WReC argues that attention to literary markets and institutions must not be "at the expense of 'literary reading.' "[4] Cheah is worried about the kind of scholarship that suggests that everything is incorporated, as though there were an evenly modernized world with markets spread out uniformly across the globe and controlled by imperializing "Western temporalities." Fair enough. Yet the urge to avoid reducing everything to capitalist commerce should not lead us to ignore the realities of production, which are after all realities not of total incorporation but of differential and uneven development and access. To ignore these realities in the name of "the literary" is more conducive to our own self-flattery than to insight.[5]

Cheah praises novels that wonderfully "map the calculations of different types of global capital and their unworlding of the world, the ruin and destruction they bring" and that "revive non-Western temporalities in the present that can aid in worlding the world otherwise." He argues that these works "foster relations of solidarity and build a shared world" (17). "The central question," he asserts, "is how subjects can be animated to change the world made by capitalist globalization and to create other worlds." He searches for a "force" that "can destabilize and disrupt the time of capital, which has become hardwired at the level of subjective consciousness" (209). Where does his search take him? To world literature. Literature may indeed have this kind of critical edge, may contain ecopolitical and anti-capitalist critique, and may help us glimpse other possible worlds. But we must at least consider the question of why, when work of this kind is so widely circulated and embraced by people within the literary milieu, the incorporative force of capitalism nevertheless motors on? To neglect this question, to ignore the delimitation of literary activity and exposure, to write as if literature is straightforwardly "an active power in the making of worlds . . . a site of processes of worlding and an agent that participates and intervenes in these processes" (Cheah 2), is to fail to recognize its actual dominant character and the contingencies and mediations that define it. Whose "worlding" does it shape? In whose thought does it intervene?

As a site of identification, style of cultural activity, and form of education, the literary tends precisely to mask the character of the primary social relations that are necessary to its own flourishing. These relations include relatively high levels of wealth, a well-funded publishing infrastructure, a forceful national copyright regime, and an accessible, state-backed educational infrastructure. High literary culture is inseparable from these social conditions. It is enabled by them and it is a form of inculcation of and engagement with the mores that they occasion. In the 1970s, Étienne Balibar and Pierre Macherey, building on work by Renée Balibar, described these mores as a bourgeois sociolect, through which those in positions of relative power seek to justify their status by claiming that they have better minds and better forms of creative expression than their inferiors.[6] The foundations of this sociolect, however, appear no longer to be in place, leaving literature with a far less assured role to play in the inculcation of dominant values. What we have now, perhaps, is the unraveling and beleaguerment of the bourgeois sociolect. What kind of literary culture emerges when the constitutive supports of high literary art have become less widespread? Whatever it is, it is something very different than what existed in the immediate postwar period. This makes it all the more remarkable that so much critical scholarly emphasis on the power of world literature—a power apparently so considerable that we are always being asked to genuflect before "the work itself" or "the aesthetic"—is emerging now, just as literary experience is becoming even more delimited than it was in the 1960s or even the 1990s. As a practice, it has become even more specialized, as literary production now takes place under conditions of decline that make it a residual rather a dominant circuit within overall cultural production.

There are remarkable parallels between Cheah's account of world literature and the role that UNESCO began to formalize for cultural policy some fifty years ago, in the late 1960s. The overlap suggests the degree of supportive convergence between a longstanding literary disposition, characterized by opposition to commodification and commercialization, and UNESCO's purview during this earlier period, when it was at its most radical as an institution. Cheah describes capitalism as the "gradual incorporation of other civilizations that were external areas as its peripheries through imperial expansion and violent colonial dispossession." Despite the violence of dispossession, these external areas "maintain their integrity" (193), and this is what culture is: the assertion of external integrity and indigeneity vis-a-vis otherwise dominant capital. Quoting the anthropologist Néstor García Canclini, Cheah writes that "the cultural domination of core countries can be resisted by reassertions of indigenous culture, because 'cultures are precisely arenas where resistance to hegemony occurs, where appeals are made to the historical value of established "civilizations" against the temporary superiorities of the market'" (193). The coincidence between this and UNESCO's policy pronouncements of the 1970s and 1980s will become clear as we proceed.

Especially during Amadou-Mahtar M'Bow's tenure as its director general (1974–1987), UNESCO devised cultural policy reflecting the idea that historical civilizations had an integral value and were in need of help in preserving their heritage against the depredation of market incorporation. UNESCO's reliance on the ongoing budget contributions of its powerful members, however, has meant that it has been forced, since the mid-1980s, to adapt to the new neoliberal times described in this book's later chapters. It has been largely compelled to embrace the mandate to be market-facing, metrics-based, and relatively nonconfrontational. It is still attached to the language of cultural particularity and harmonious difference within universality, but its moment of anti-capitalist vibrancy has faded away to almost nothing. Particularity and difference, though always presented as the building blocks of any cultural value, have now in some respects become precisely what Cheah is eager to malign in his treatment: commodities and tourist attractions.

How then to explain Cheah's—and WReC's—holding on to literature as a source of uniquely powerful evidence of what remains precapitalist, integrally different, "external" to capitalism? Literary scholars within universities were protected, until more recently, from the forces that came to change UNESCO, and it is the severity of the threats they now face that has induced them to cling to the idealization of literature as a potent site of noncommercial humanistic social formation. The very precariousness of English literary studies leads to an insistence on its propitious politics and salvific social role—the desperate search for what Cheah calls a "normative worldly force immanent to literature."

And yet if, as the study of UNESCO suggests, a global high-literary milieu has in fact been part of the culture of a particular phase in the history of bourgeois social formation, that milieu is likely to continue to crumble along with its key foundations: a robust system of higher education and liberal democracy. Cheah wants literature to "animate" "subjects" who are able to "change the world," but one guesses it will be other factors—the growing divide between the uber-rich and the rest of the world, declining workforce participation and an expanding untaxed informal sector, the further erosion of state-based social provisions, and climate transformation and the depletion of nature's reserves—that will feature in the demise of capitalism. None of this is to say that literature will play no role in how people envision what comes next. But its future normative force is not something we can or need to specify in the present.

What we can specify is how any such potential normative force is mediated and corralled. In its raucous 1970s heyday, UNESCO supported the extension of a decommodified cultural sphere that would be actively protected by government funding from total reliance on direct market sales. But at the same time, UNESCO also backed something else that Cheah sidelines: insight into the unevenness and inequities of cultural production. UNESCO's attention to precapitalist cultural formations and ungovernable polities was not at the level of a thematic representation or formal analysis of what arises from the multiplicity of temporalities, but had to do instead with how the global cultural milieu was controlled by acquisitive hegemonic forces: content-producing Americans, white people of European origins, the dominant copyright holders whose material and cultural wealth positioned them as benevolent distributors of technical assistance and humanitarian aid.

UNESCO's work at this time also partook of and supported the Marxist materialist sociology of literature that was emerging in parallel, in work by figures such as Raymond Williams, Stuart Hall, Pierre Macherey, Jean Franco, Renée Balibar, and Étienne Balibar. In the late 1960s, UNESCO published writers like Pierre Bourdieu, Lucien Goldmann, and Georg Lukács in its own journal, *International Social Science*, in special issues on the "Social Functions of Education" and "Sociology of Literary Creativity." In 1968, Richard Hoggart, who had been heading the Birmingham Centre for Cultural Studies, took up a position at UNESCO, to be succeeded in Birmingham by Stuart Hall. These are just a few examples of UNESCO's strong connection with that cultural sphere; I discuss others throughout these pages. At the time, in the late 1960s and throughout the 1970s, many of UNESCO's own highest executives were scholars and researchers. In addition, many sociologists and proto-sociologists advised UNESCO and wrote reports and books with its backing. They spoke at UNESCO-backed conferences on the role of art in society, on how to support indigenous cultural production in the underdeveloped world, on problems of neocolonial dependence, and so on. It is this original cultural sociology, most of it explicitly Marxist in orientation, that continues to motivate and inform my work. I rely on it extensively here. Its foundational methodological claims about the entanglements of power, culture, and capitalism retain their salience today, because the underlying economic conditions animating that scholarship continue in force in their inexorable way. They continue in force, that is, but in novel guises that ground new entanglements of culture and power and new kinds of production of literary culture.

There is a considerable scholarship addressing official institutional attempts to use literature and culture for social and political ends. The cultural Cold War waged by the United States, with the high-level drama of CIA backing, is by far the most studied nexus, featured in works by Frances Stonor Saunders, Greg Barnhisel, and Eric Bennett, among others. These scholars agree that the elite culture associated with artistic autonomy and experimentation was exported by the United States as evidence of American freedoms. Merve Emre has recently stressed, somewhat differently, that in their efforts to spread the ideology of American democracy, US institutions fostered "bad" or inexpert acts of reading. These took place not in university classrooms but at events sponsored by institutions interested in literature as a form of public communication, such as those held under the auspices of Eisenhower's People-to-People Initiative, which sent writers on global lecture and reading tours.[7] Literature was part of the cultural material that was supposed to help people around the world acclimate to US hegemony and take the right position in support of Cold War liberalism. Reading was meant to be instruction in the virtues of American culture, and American writers were presented to international audiences as living proof of their country's greatness.

There were struggling and disaffected populations to be managed at home in the United States as well, and by the late 1960s the global periphery was competing for funding priority with American inner cities. Stephen Schryer has uncovered the extensive cultural programming attached to the Johnson administration's War on Poverty. This programming ended up backing the development of expressions of radical black art, which proved to be a square peg for the round hole of state prerogatives. Karen Ferguson, in turn, emphasizes where wealthy white interests did triumph, as the Ford Foundation worked to quiet radical black politics in America's inner cities during the crisis that unfolded beginning in the late 1960s. As prospects for impoverished black people in inner cities deteriorated, the Ford Foundation further emphasized elite high-art development and individual upward mobility, including backing the Black Arts movement and the development of Black Studies programs at universities.[8]

I have mentioned here just a few of the more insightful studies of how US-based state programs, and private funders working in allegiance with state programs, have used literature and culture to achieve social and political goals that include the containment of radical political currents and the channeling of experiences of social instability and unease away from more conflictual responses and toward the ostensibly pacifying activity of culture making. A substantial body of research in critical cultural policy studies, largely informed by Michel Foucault's work on the disciplining of subjects, takes a similar approach. This body of research considers how governments have used culture as suasion and pacification, and it understands cultural policy as "a means of governance, of formatting public collective subjectivity."[9]

These are fruitful frameworks for thinking about UNESCO. Some of its dominant rationales for cultural policy making have been securing adherence to liberal democratic capitalism and helping people manage living in immiserated conditions. Yet one outcome of the international and historical sweep of my research, considering UNESCO from its founding right up until the present, is a deeper sense of how the logic of instrumentalization has changed with the tides of global economic development and integration. The global cultural policy milieu has shifted its emphases as the postwar hegemony of the United States and expansive capitalist development have emerged. That policy milieu has been indelibly shaped by the fitful incorporation of postcolonial regions that rarely managed to achieve the development and dynamism some sought, and whose interests in cultural programming differed markedly from those of the United States and the other advanced economies. It has also been affected by the climate of austerity, resource exhaustion, and new forms of imperialist extraction and exploitation that characterize our contemporary zero-sum moment.

UNESCO's Literary Programs and the Global Economy: An Overview

Three signal phases in UNESCO's history can be identified quite readily. The first was the immediate postwar moment, which was dominated by a liberal cosmopolitan worldview pitted against the threat of fascism, communism, and totalitarianism. The next was the 1960s and 1970s, when many of the newly postcolonial nations had joined UN agencies and gained a platform within those agencies, which then became significantly focused on economic development and rectifying inequality in living standards (by the end of the 1970s, in fact, both the United Nations and UNESCO were consumed by the concerns generated by a series of economic crises and a growing fear that fair global economic integration for the developing nations was a pipe dream). The final phase has unfolded from about the mid-1980s on, when UNESCO had to win back its major funders, which had withdrawn from the organization, and when the realities of global economic turbulence and stagnation had become hard to ignore; during this phase, culture became tied ever more expressly to goals of productivity and growth, leading into our era of faith in the unique dynamism of the so-called creative economy.

Though UNESCO has used books in dozens of its endeavors, there have been three major book industry programs corresponding to and crystallizing the three historical phases. The first program was the UNESCO Collection of Representative Works, which was created to support the translation and cross-border dissemination of the world's classic literature. This program emerged during the founding of the organization, after World War II, when UNESCO was dominated by the United States, Britain, and France and was explicitly directed to support the spread of liberal capitalist democracy. It treated books as objects of diplomacy whose exchange would foster cultural understanding. The second program was 1972's International Book Year, which emerged with the rise of a new majority within UNESCO made up of the recently decolonized and anti-colonial nations. This program reflected a broader movement toward treatment of the book not as an object of portable elite cultural knowledge but instead as an agent of social and economic change in the developing world. The third program entailed granting cities the status of City of Literature; it was connected to the promotion of World Book and Copyright Day and to the establishment of UNESCO's Creative Cities Network. These movements started to emerge in the 1990s and reflect a move toward thinking of books as part of a brandable national cultural heritage and creative economy.

The immediate postwar period, a time of economic expansion, was also a moment of extensive direct investment in culture, entailing massive UNESCO projects to write exhaustive global histories of knowledge, religion, and so on. A major motivation for cultural projects at this time was to enable the continued spread of liberal capitalist democracy. People involved in UNESCO's early formation and operations, such as Julian Huxley, who was its first director general, and Archibald MacLeish, the United States Librarian of Congress at the time and a member of UNESCO's executive council, were deeply concerned about the transition from the age of empire to the age of fragmentation. They worried about how to establish a unified global vision that could combat the threats of disintegration and Soviet takeover. What helps to explain UNESCO's programming during its first few decades, when its official slogan was "peace in the minds of men," was the desire to set the stage for the continued construction of a truly thriving global economy organized under US hegemony. The idea was to create conditions that would encourage direct foreign investment and allow businesses to realize their productive capacities through expansion. Paired with these desires was anxiety over how to establish unity in the wake of the dissolution of Europe's formal empires, to support what Huxley approvingly dubbed "white capitalist expansion" or what Arthur Schlesinger Jr. would soon call "the vital center"—a center best provided, he thought, by an internationally directed and enlightened liberal version of American society.[10]

The first two chapters of this book are an account of the earliest period of UNESCO's formation. They interpret the Collection of Representative Works in relation to the fear of global disintegration that motivated Huxley and many of his peers. Yasunari Kawabata was the head of the Japanese branch of PEN International in the early 1950s when his novel *Snow Country* was recommended for inclusion in the program. He was a key figure within a global literary community that embraced cosmopolitan liberalism. This community hoped, with the help of agencies like PEN and UNESCO, to support the creation of a realm of elite aesthetic expression. They wanted to be "above" politics and were wary of wars and of authoritarian governments, but they also respected the sovereignty of nations and were committed to the idea of local particularity and tradition as forming the foundation of renewable cultural wealth. This is the same cultural wealth that UNESCO would soon devote itself to highlighting and then enduringly "safeguarding." The English translation of *Snow Country*, published in 1956 as part of Alfred A. Knopf's important series of translations of Japanese literature, embodies the aesthetic ideology and general world view espoused by the American development establishment and by UNESCO at the time. In the novel, folk traditions are encountered and preserved as a sign of the enlightened cosmopolitanism of an intellectual elite seeking to secure its dominance.

UNESCO's postwar policy-making activity reflected and supported developments within its member nations. Within the United States, large amounts of state and private foundation money—via the Ford Foundation and the CIA-backed Congress for Cultural Freedom, for example—went to cultural endeavors in support of a pro-American, pro-development, pro-capitalist world view. In the United Kingdom, the famous welfarist economist John Maynard Keynes himself played a role in founding the Arts Council of Great Britain, which has even been described as his reward for "his services as economic strategist to the nation."[11] Meanwhile, the spread of US hegemony occasioned attempts, such as Canada's Massey Commission, to support arts that might otherwise have been subsumed by the American mass culture monolith.[12] Across the developed economies, in fact, the establishment of official cultural policy, for the first time coordinating and institutionalizing formerly haphazard state patronage, was closely linked to the general effort to secure full employment, to reward workers for their loyalty by providing social programs, and to increase educational opportunities. It was enabled by the economic dynamism of the immediate postwar period.

This dynamism eventually slowed, however, giving way to the era of economic crises. At UNESCO during this period, which lasted, roughly, from the late 1960s through the early 1980s, we find the balance of power, and control over major debates, shifting to favor new Third World member nations. Cultural policy was especially embattled during this period, as there existed for the first time a concerted effort to define and devise cultural policy mandates for the developing world. Suffering economies were no longer willing to take their contribution to UNESCO's budget for granted. They threatened to withdraw when their preferences did not sufficiently inform policy. At the same time, UNESCO became the staging ground for many debates about the nature of American cultural imperialism and the depredations of the "free market." Within these debates there arose an alternative emphasis on human-focused development, often discussed under the rubric of "cultural development." Chapters 3 and 4 argue that deliberate articulation of the value of cultural policy arises at this moment precisely in response to the fallout from global economic decline. The formal cultural policy discussions that took place across the period were one mechanism through which the new postcolonial member nations took advantage of the crises of legitimacy plaguing the developed-economy states. They stressed values that had been threatened or eviscerated by the developed capitalist economies that had dominated UNESCO to date, and they promoted their own ostensibly fairer and more "balanced" approaches to the integration of new enclaves into the global economic order. Chapter 3 concludes with a discussion of Tayeb Salih's "The Doum Tree of Wad Hamid," a story that illuminates the perils of integration into capitalist modernity. Salih spent much of his professional life in cultural policy work, including at UNESCO, and his tale of the doum tree shows how a precapitalist community responds to its culture becoming subject to heritage preservation. It is a widely known story, much beloved and written about by people interested in narratives of development, and yet none have recognized it as a fantasy designed to complement and reinforce emerging cultural policy mandates.

At the United Nations during this same period (the late 1960s through the early 1980s), postcolonial member nations were pushing for the codification of a new international economic order. At UNESCO at the same time, a new world information and communications order was envisioned. These policy debates were meant to result in guidelines that would provide a foundation for establishing fairer conditions for developing nations eager to expand their local cultural production capacities. The representatives from these nations were for the most part not opposed to economic development, but they recognized its risks and wanted a greater role in controlling how development occurred. In designating 1972 as International Book Year, UNESCO's postcolonial member nations argued not just for the expansion of publishing industries but for the right to tell their own stories and be heard. Growth in the publishing sector was thereby yoked to a humanizing anti-imperialism and to the discourse of human rights. In *The Book Hunger*, published by UNESCO, Ronald Barker and Robert

Escarpit claimed that the developing world was suffering from a hunger for books as the result of underdeveloped local productive capacity, left over from the colonial era. They and others argued that this hunger was exacerbated by the ongoing media dominance of the developed economies, and further stymied by foreign book donation schemes, which were especially rampant due to Cold War funding for propaganda from both the United States and the Soviet Union. Representatives from the developing nations spoke of expanding local capacity to compete against those dominating the global market, and of wanting to serve local audiences otherwise dependent on foreign content. The United States and Britain, however, opposed these policy developments, with considerable success, not least because the United States controlled 25 percent of UNESCO's budget and was often on the brink of withdrawing its membership. Meanwhile, developed-world media companies actively lobbied against anything that might threaten their dominance.

UNESCO's history as a site of contestation during this period complicates claims that UN agencies have served to straightforwardly incorporate postcolonial and precapitalist enclaves into global capitalism. Scholars such as Giovanni Arrighi, Gilbert Rist, and Konstantina Tzouvala have argued that for postcolonial nations to be active members of the new international order represented by the United Nations, they needed to be perceptibly engaged in the establishment of global trade relations and the abolition of precapitalist relations of production. These scholars have suggested that decolonization entailed the establishment of sovereign statehood, and that sovereign statehood in turn secured an international legal order inseparable from the development of capitalist social relations.[13] It has even been argued that the whole UN system has mainly served as an extension of American hegemony or a wing of the American state.[14] And yet, while there is some truth to these sweeping assessments, they do not sufficiently explain UNESCO's programming from the late 1960s through the early 1980s, when that programming most reflected and fostered a concern with the very nature of modernization and development—what it is that they threaten and erase. There was no easy adherence to developmentalism at UNESCO, and this is key.

UNESCO has in fact become one of the premiere sites where a dispositional wariness towards capitalist modernization and development attends any kind of cultural policy making and gate keeping—and, indeed, liberal bourgeois power in general. The global literary milieu, with which UNESCO is consistently allied, is another site where this disposition has been formed. Its characteristic ambivalence features a critique of what is castigated as purely economically motivated development and a caution against or lament over the integration of precapitalist enclaves—the erasure of communal social relations and the threats to cultural monuments and to any values that prove to be incompatible with modernizing drives. As a staging ground for the elaboration of this ambivalence, UNESCO has offered the intellectuals affiliated with it a space in which to register the threats and depredations that arise with capitalist development. Even now, when some form of development is embraced, whether it is welcomed or simply acknowledged as inevitable, UNESCO policy makers will argue that it must occur in a humanized form if it is to contribute to the goals of enlightened social organization, progress, and real peace among nations. Those who rally around cultural economies often use precisely such language, presenting culture as a limitless resource whose marketization can easily be made ethically sound and universally beneficial. We cannot understand what cultural policy is without understanding how its formation reflects and codifies this primary ambivalence about the extent to which economic development "alone" is conducive to human flourishing.

In other words, while it is no doubt true that postwar cultural policy as an aspect of governance is an extension of elite bourgeois liberal power, it is also the case that it has tended to be a highly involved and often ambivalent mode of engagement with the economic conditions that subtend this power. It has tended to reflect the faith that there are values that transcend and should contextualize and humanize commodity cultures and capitalist social relations. The expression of this faith, however, has constantly shifted, for reasons that we can readily observe and explain. In the immediate postwar period, an emphasis on ineffable, nonquantifiable, and noninstrumental values was a means of justifying the export of liberal capitalist democracies as model polities because they ostensibly allow culture this kind of freedom. In the decolonizing middle period, it was a way of encouraging the developed economies to respect and answer to the demands of the new postcolonial states who sought to counter the dominance of the advanced economies by insisting on their own superior grasp of culture's "humanizing" potential. Finally, most recently, trumpeting the value of what cannot be quantified is a clear means of encouraging consumers to spend their leisure budgets on UNESCO-branded heritage experiences and encouraging member nations, in spite of their own conditions of austerity, to continue to invest some of what they have left for social spending in the chimera of the infinitely expandable and humanely organized creative economy.

We know that the arguments that UNESCO advanced during this postcolonial period, in favor of redistributed cultural wealth and humanized development, had little impact on the actual state of the global economy. The advanced economies were to remain the source of development, through state-based technical training and assistance as well as private investment and development aid programs. There was no real mitigation of dependence nor of global economic unevenness. As a result, the developing economies were not able to devote the levels of funding to cultural production that would have been necessary to really address any so-called cultural hunger. The dominant nations within UNESCO worked hard to ensure that the developing-world members did not pose even a minor threat to their control over the making and dissemination of intellectual property. Pittance wages, unemployment, and informal-sector work are not conducive to healthy state coffers. Instead, decolonization produced what Nancy Fraser has called "low-value postcolonial citizenship," in which peripheral or surplus people are technically outside the wage nexus but are exploited by other means, and their communally held social wealth, such as that found in cultural practices that have been developed into heritage and tourism experiences, is expropriated rather than being cultivated in ways that benefit local populations.[15]

By the early 1980s, the dream of a unified and ultra-prosperous Third World seemed highly fantastical. It is telling that one of the events that UNESCO sponsored in the 1970s was the Second World Black and African Festival of Arts and Culture, or FESTAC, held in Lagos in 1977. The festival was funded mainly by petrodollars. It clearly used culture, especially spectacularized precolonial folk traditions, to sell Nigeria as the petrol-rich king of African nations: open for business. A comparison could be made with the ongoing annual Smithsonian Folklife Festival, where regions continue to present sanitized versions of their national folk traditions to attract tourists and other kinds of foreign investment. There is authentic local production being safeguarded in these contexts, but it is staged in order to induce global trade, with culture playing a very particular role as an industry that is itself ready for development and whose spectacular forms are also able to sell investment in the region in general. In simpler terms, FESTAC was part of an attempt to siphon petrodollars into foreign investment in Nigeria, and to this end it licensed a certain amount of local cultural production in the hopes that circulation of culture would induce economic activity more broadly.[16] The UNESCO imprimatur aided in the effort to produce the legitimacy of the

Nigerian state. At the same time, it entailed the production of the legitimacy of UNESCO as a global cultural institution.

FESTAC took place as the global economic downturn was already underway. It assigned to the performance of local culture the kind of protagonism more usually associated with the neoliberal creative-economy age, tying the construction of cultural institutions in Lagos to a vibrant national brand and to efforts to imagine and thereby drive a thriving economy. In the third and final phase of cultural policy making, the FESTAC approach has become the norm. From our present vantage, debates over corporate media, global economic imbalances, and humanized capitalism seem like remnants of a more politically dynamic time, full of possibility. The neoliberal governance that had started to become the dominant global arrangement by the late 1980s utterly transformed UNESCO, which soon came to use cultural programming mainly to prop up local industries and generate tourism and trade. How does the increasing economic power of the creative industries, along with governments' clear interest in measuring and supporting this power, relate to the broader context of economic contraction? Chapters 5 and 6 tackle this question.

In part it is simply that culture means employment for people who would otherwise be out of work. It is a sector from which some profits can be extracted when other sectors are not viable. UNESCO policies now also actively position creative industries as having a role to play in fostering a harmonious social body by mitigating unease. Where direct conflict is kept at bay, there is more likely to be a willingness to invest in local businesses, insure public infrastructure projects, and set up shop in an area where insurance will be available. Ultimately, the social role of culture is also economic, in that the amelioration of social conflict, and the potential for culture to soothe many personal and social strains, provide a more successful environment for commerce.[17] Policy making for the creative industries is often directed toward all these ends. It is about trying to build competitive national economies in hard times, when there are vast unemployed populations dispossessed by global economic policies or reliant on abysmally paid and insecure employment. Creative-economy frameworks bring diverse practices involving intellectual property production together under one patentable umbrella or sellable formula that is ready for export and for expert application, usually by consultants. They "create partnerships." They "bring private- and public-sector actors together." They imagine and disseminate plans for the growth of a matrix defined by market-facing creativity and innovation supports.

This most recent stage in UNESCO's history is thus largely given over to creative-economy boosterism. What we see in UNESCO's specifically literary programming, such as its branding of Cities of Literature, is the belief that literature has become what cultural sociologists studying the literary field have called "an object of cultural consumption for dwindling and aging publics."[18] These publics have levels of education in the humanities and of leisure and income that are not so much in evidence in younger generations—and, when they are, mainly as a niche instance, a sort of hipster localism connected to the cultivation of creative-industries workforces who are attracted to independent café-cum-bookstores as lifestyle amenities. In the contemporary period, UNESCO's policy with respect to literary works has largely been to brand the best instances and then leave them to their own devices, as literary culture is assumed to be supported by an audience that is unusual in its composition. UNESCO now devotes more resources, especially in the developing economies, to what are thought to be emergent, more accessible, and more racially diverse cultural forms, such as music and digital cultural production. These resources are invested in culture as a possible way of creating careers and money for people in stagnant economies and as a set of affective experiences with the potential to forge bonds that will make for a stable polity. Chapter 5 discusses Zakes Mda's 2000 novel *The Heart of Redness* in this context. The novel exemplifies the sort of fantasy of a sustainable, locally directed, cultural industry that UNESCO policy currently embraces. As a novel, it is actively designed to counsel an elite niche of cultural workers who will themselves ultimately be devoted not to literary activity—far too rarefied—but to more accessible forms of cultural production, like heritage tourism. It fosters faith in authentic cultural activities as sites of both enlivening experience and economic dynamism.

Lately, when UNESCO does support the book trades, it is through mechanisms such as copyright enforcement in underdeveloped markets. This differs dramatically from UNESCO's earlier history of engagement with the inequities of copyright provision. Chapter 6 begins with a discussion of UNESCO's funding for ZIMCOPY, an initiative to crack down on piracy in the Zimbabwean book trades. It concludes with a discussion of the way in which NoViolet Bulawayo's 2013 novel, *We Need New Names*, responds to the persistence and deepening of conditions of maldistribution, and so provides a unique window onto UNESCO's support for strong measures against book pirates. *We Need New Names* assumes that its readers, probably unusually wealthy and highly educated, will be unlike its characters, who are forced to sell images of their own suffering in order to receive charity. It thus unsettles the idea that the development of a substantial literary industry in Zimbabwe, signified by paperbound books produced by incorporated commercial publishers, will simply and naturally result from the penalizing of book pirates. Who, after all, would buy these books? *We Need New Names* also sides with those who do technically "criminal" things in order to survive—a fit summation of the contemporary condition of the literary book in Zimbabwe and elsewhere.

UNESCO's Collection of Representative Works

UNESCO'S FIRST MAJOR LITERARY PROGRAM, the Collection of Representative Works, was proposed by the Lebanese National Committee in UNESCO's earliest days. The original idea behind the program, as expressed in the program proposal presented to the UN, was that "the translation and dissemination of the great works of all nations are a powerful means of promoting international exchange likely to increase the mutual knowledge and understanding of peoples and so contribute to the maintenance of peace and security."[1] The project of bringing the world's most notable literatures together onto a global roster of masterworks was intended to foster cross-cultural understanding and help to establish the bases of lasting world peace.

The Collection of Representative Works still exists. Though it now supports the translation of a wide variety of types of writing, including contemporary literature, its first focus was exclusively classics, defined as works published before 1900, accessible to a general audience, "bear[ing] witness to the state of civilization" and taking their "place in the history of culture." Classics chosen for the program would, "while revealing the human aspects of national culture, simultaneously bring out the unity and brotherhood of man."[2] Some of the classics brought into the program have been translated into "languages of little diffusion"; in addition, the Lebanese committee that first proposed the program promoted translation into Arabic and took the free movement of works into and out of that language to be a crucial measure of Lebanon's modernity. Still, most translation has been into French or English. UNESCO's initial plans for the program in fact suggest that "as a contribution to universal culture," priority should be accorded to translation into the "main cultural tongues."[3]

The records of the first meeting of the United Nations General Assembly refer to a discussion of the Collection of Representative Works. The program is described as being intended to entail a significant level of translation of the classics "deemed by the highest authorities to have universal significance and permanent value" into languages that are spoken in nations that in fact "do not have sufficient facilities and resources for the authentic translation of numerous classics into their languages." The records state further that "such translation is greatly conducive to their cultural development."[4] On the basis of this initial plan, which was never quite realized in this form, the General Assembly referred the matter of the Collection of Representative Works to the United Nations Economic and Social Council for further scrutiny. The Economic and Social Council subsequently asked UNESCO to submit, by June 1, 1948, a report, "including particularly data on objective methods of selection of great books, the needs of various cultural regions, and suggestions for general assistance in translation, publication and distribution."[5] This resulted in a substantial document presented for the council's consideration.

The nature of the document indicates that defining a classic and preparing lists of classic works for translation was an immense undertaking and an important part of UNESCO's initial activities. Before preparing the report, UNESCO had already written to the governments of member states, asking them to inform the UNESCO Secretariat "of the official and private bodies, associations and persons in their countries best fitted to supply the necessary information."[6] It received replies from Australia, Belgium, Bolivia, Canada, France, Norway, Siam, the United Kingdom, and Venezuela. Using those replies, UNESCO staff then compiled a list of individuals and institutions, including universities as well as other academic bodies and learned societies, and sent a questionnaire to each.

The preamble to the questionnaire states that UNESCO takes a classic to be "any work, in whatever intellectual field . . . which is deemed representative of a culture or a nation and which remains as a landmark in the cultural history of mankind." It goes on to say that, though "it may express a particular culture, it is a characteristic of a classic that it transcends the limits of that culture and is representative of it, not only within the nation itself, but also in the eyes of other nations." It must have "stood the test of time and have preserved [its] human value for generations." It states moreover that UNESCO will only publish those works which "no excessive difficulty of wording or meaning puts out of reach of a broadly educated and well-read public." The questionnaire itself then asks what works are "classics," but beyond that, also asks which of those works deemed classics "do you consider: (a) the most accessible to the rest of the world ('universal')? (b) the most representative of your culture and national genius?"

Respondents are further asked which works they deem most worthy of translation, in order of priority; they are also asked to look beyond the nation to write a "universal list including the classics of all ages and all countries," and to rank "100 of these in order of priority"; they are asked if there are works that have already been translated but that need retranslating; they are asked to draw up another list in order of priority of all works that should be translated; and finally, they are asked for the names of the best translators "at your country's service for the accomplishment of this task."[7]

The questionnaire was sent to those individuals and organizations originally suggested by the member nations who had sent in their surveys. Concurrently, because not all works, and especially not works in dead languages, are the recognized property of one particular modern nation, it was also sent to nongovernmental organizations, including PEN International, the International Commission on the History of Literature, the International Council of Scientific Unions, the International Union for the History of Science, the World Federation of Scientific Workers, and the International Institute of Philosophy. Given the onerous quantity of work that the questionnaire asked respondents to undertake, it is perhaps no surprise that at the time of the preparation of the report for the Economic and Social Council, in June 1948, only three had been filled out and returned: one originating in Belgium, one in Austria, and one in the United Kingdom.

But UNESCO had also convened an international committee of experts for a meeting in Paris to be held in May 1948. The report that was presented to the United Nations Economic and Social Council relies heavily on the views of the experts who attended that meeting, which included Alan Lane (a British publisher and cofounder of Penguin Books), V. S. Pritchett (a British writer and literary critic), Taha Hussein (an Egyptian writer and intellectual who was a figurehead for Arabic literary modernism), and Frederic Melcher (an American publisher, editor, bookseller, and libraries expert). In the report, the definition of a classic is reiterated. A classic "bears witness to the state of civilization and can take its place in the history of culture"; it was written before 1900; and ideally, "while revealing the human aspects of national culture, simultaneously bring[s] out the unity and brotherhood of man." Its audience is neither scholars nor the masses, but the "generally educated public, for the development and increase of which this project is in fact designed." The committee recommended edited anthologies and collections of selected works for this reason: such texts avoid the "appearance of difficulty to a public of a different culture." It advised that a first list of seventy-five works "regarded as universal classics" be drawn up and submitted to all parties for comment before any decision was made as to a final list of a total of about a hundred world classics.[8]

The committee also recommended that each national committee set up a translation subcommittee, consisting of writers, scientists, and philosophers "representative of the various currents of thought in their different fields." It should also include publishers or others familiar with problems of translation, publishing, and dissemination. These subcommittees would work with a permanent UNESCO committee, the International Committee for Translations, made up of relevant representatives from the publishing world and translation specialists. It would meet once a year and consult with international agencies to ensure that ancient languages and works from nonmember nations be included. A permanent special committee within UNESCO would be tasked with drawing up and maintaining the lists of works for translation. First priority would be given to the translation of the long list of all recognized classics into two or three "main cultural tongues" "as a contribution to universal culture"; the second task would be a short list of a small number of classics for translation into "the greatest number of tongues," "as a contribution to the development of cultures at present least favoured."[9] That the first task became so overwhelmingly dominant is a sign of the sheer force within UNESCO of the French and English languages. It is also a sign of the persistent underdevelopment of the cultural infrastructures that would have supported substantial literary translation projects among the "least favoured" cultures.

The report does not ignore the practical difficulties of publishing and disseminating translated works. It suggests that the works be inexpensive, manufactured in a convenient trim size, and have a "high-standard" appearance—a specification that already privileges the book industries of the developed world. It also suggests that these publications provide helpful guidance for readers, such as "informative rather than critical" introductions, and annotations where needed. In the initial proposal, most funding was to come not from UNESCO's own base budget but from the state or states from which a given translation project arose (for instance through bulk purchases for libraries and schools or the setting aside of a "reasonable proportion of the [rationed] paper at their disposal for the printing of translated classics") as well as from foundations, learned societies, and the publishers themselves. UNESCO's role would be to help publishers by providing the list of works and the list of translators. It would also offer further support through publicity, allowing publishers to "distinguish satisfactory translations by a symbol constituting an adequate guarantee for the reader and encouragement to him to buy and read the book." The UNESCO brand would point out the "world-wide nature of the undertaking."[10]

In the end, the first project consisted of the translation into English, French, and Spanish of works by Al-Ghazali and the translation into French alone of works by Avicenna, as well as the translation into Arabic of Dante's *Divine Comedy*, Aristotle's *Politics*, Cervantes's *Don Quixote*, Shakespeare's *A Winter's Tale*, Bacon's *Essays*, Descartes's *Discours de la méthode*, and Manzoni's *Storia della colonna infame*. This first project took place under the auspices of the International Commission for the Translation of Great Books, which was founded in Beirut by the Lebanese government and UNESCO. The second project was the translation of Latin American works written in Spanish and Portuguese—the first an anthropology of Mexican poetry—into French and English under the auspices of the Organization of American States.[11]

Over the years, sponsored works have been released as co-editions with partner publishing firms, including some at the vanguard of large-scale global publishing, such as Macmillan. More common, though, are arrangements with firms that have a reputation as being elite and noncommercial, such as Columbia University Press, Grove Press, Alfred A. Knopf, and The Bodley Head. To date, the catalog contains more than thirteen hundred titles from more than eighty countries, translated from a hundred or so languages. Though the program has moved away from the exclusive focus on works published prior to 1900, later discussions of its mission have not substantially departed from the initial focus on a work's unique local origins coupled with its legibility to a universal community. Discussing "World Literary Values" at the Federation of Translators in 1985, a Polish translator involved with the program described UNESCO as preserving "the treasures of world classical literature and the highest attainment of contemporary writers," who, like Shakespeare, Dickens, and Tolstoy, embody "the life of their own people and . . . epoch."[12] She suggested that UNESCO's task is to establish cultural ambassadors to provide a "fuller and more vivid picture of life in distant or unknown lands," a picture that is "no less moving than an exotic voyage" but is seen through eyes that are more "penetrating" than the "naked and unprepared eyes of the tourist."[13]

UNESCO's own commentary on and guidelines for the Collection of Representative Works have continued to state that works must serve as a "reflection of a specific community or civilization." To be included in the program, a work must be "known and acknowledged in the community in which it was created" and already have "full visibility and credibility in its original region."[14] What is important is that a certain community of experts have loyalty to the work. Its regional visibility is the criterion for its subsidized access to a larger sphere. Much as with later programs devised to preserve humanity's tangible and intangible heritage—the Lists of Intangible Cultural Heritage, for example, and the attendant management of World Heritage Sites—selection for the Collection of Representative Works entails becoming part of a permanent archive of items deemed worthy of a global community's attention.

* * *

At the time of its establishment, one of the forces driving the Collection of Representative Works was UNESCO's general interest in the compilation and publication of a comprehensive survey of the scientific and cultural heritage of all mankind. Recording in a few languages everything ever known was supposed to foster the coming of an international consciousness. The fact that the foundation of this cosmopolitan consciousness would mostly involve the movement of materials from around the world into a few centralized Western storehouses was not considered a problem but was rather a key and determining feature of the enterprise.

Julian Huxley, the brother of the literary futurologist Aldous Huxley, believed that before real equality could be achieved, the underdeveloped world would have to be "brought up" to the standards set by the more powerful economies, via a general uplift that combined economic, social, political, and cultural transformation. His personal philosophy, which he called transhumanism, was grounded in the idea that international cooperation in forwarding knowledge about science and technology was the best basis for collectively willed and controlled progress toward a suprahuman sphere of perfect achievement. Furthering human evolution required the accumulation of all knowledge traditions in a UNESCO-like central location or storehouse accessible to all. An encyclopedia of everything ever known would foster the coming of international consciousness, and this consciousness, which could only be secured thanks to movement toward a uniform standard of material comfort, was what would secure lasting peace. The place of the arts in this process was not, for Huxley, equal to that of the sciences. They would instead help to envisage the mutual understanding that would lay the groundwork for world political unity and suprahumanity.[15] And while people from the developing world would certainly participate in this progressive evolution, they would do so largely as recipients of Western imperial largess—at least until the living standards of the abysmally poor had changed such that they would be able to develop significant scientific and technical wealth of their own.

An emphasis on the connection between social and cultural tendencies on the one hand and economic and political foundations on the other was especially welcome at UNESCO. It was, after all, first and foremost a cultural organization with a limited mandate, though it wanted to assume a broader and more important role in bringing about the conditions conducive to global peace and general prosperity. The preamble to UNESCO's constitution states that "a peace based exclusively upon the political and economic arrangements of governments would not be a peace which could secure the unanimous, lasting and sincere support of the peoples of the world, and that the peace must therefore be founded, if it is not to fail, upon the intellectual and moral solidarity of mankind."[16] Sustained human development would entail change that was not just political and economic but intellectual and moral.

Such thinking was to become crucial to the powerful developmentalist ethos that defined mainstream social science and the US foreign policy establishment in the 1950s and 1960s, when much evidence was gathered to support claims that an individual's personality fundamentally derived from their overall socio-cultural situation. Compare UNESCO's preamble to President Harry Truman's Point Four Program, a pillar of the development age that US representatives to UNESCO would take as a model for their own activity.[17] Point Four focused on raising living standards under the crucial stewardship of US expertise, backed by the uniquely prosperous postwar US economy. Truman's 1949 inaugural address, announcing the program, affirmed America's commitment to the United Nations and vowed to "embark on a bold new program for making the benefits of our scientific advances and industrial progress available for the improvement and growth of underdeveloped areas."[18] United States-based developmentalism supposed, as did UNESCO, that a society's economic and political modernization were inseparable from the enlightened transformation of its social and cultural mores. UNESCO intellectuals rejected the biological determinism of fascist Nazis, arguing instead that individuals are shaped less by inescapable physiological traits than by shifting social and cultural patterning, which would be redirected in the inevitable course of modernization. What appeared to be the fundaments of a society—a preference for communal over individual identity, for example, or small subsistence farming over large-scale agricultural schemes— could change given the right conditions.

* * *

Art and culture would be asked to play supporting roles to the dramatic transformations of the development process. Huxley's own belief was that classic works of beauty produced by "primitive" peoples who were threatened but had not yet been debased by mass commercialism, Western civilization, and the tourist trade in "curios" were the best antidote to the negative repercussions of an otherwise necessary and laudable process of modernization.[19] I focus on Huxley here not because he was singularly influential within UNESCO but because he was a prolific writer and because his thinking is so symptomatic of the currents at work within the Collection of Representative Works and within the intellectual community more generally at the time. Huxley's tendency was to position the world beyond "the West" as a source for works with a holistic, community-forming function rejected by modernist writers. He saw London, for instance, as a place in need of social management: its people suffered from an industrial urban malaise; bad design was everywhere; its natural environment had been spoiled; and its architecture was increasingly shoddy. Literature was to ameliorate these ills, and it deserved support from state programs when it helped the citizenry ease frustration and stave off unhappiness and unrest. He found it unfortunate that most Western art refused to do anything of the sort. Lamenting that the artist in the developed world does not represent "something essential in the life of the community," he noted that it had grown "in upon itself, to become esoteric, incomprehensible except to the self-chosen clique."[20]

Such thinking clearly informed the way that the Collection of Representative Works was imagined and instituted. Supported works had to be obviously enlivening; they must not exclude their audiences; and they had to be widely accessible. Huxley wanted UNESCO to facilitate the storage and exchange of things that were more integrally human. For him, the literature most worthy of transnational circulation was that which served as a repository of the residual values of holistic community, characterized as not primarily market-oriented and uncorrupted by commerce, as non-technocratic and nonscientific.

Yet in his short book on UNESCO's purpose and philosophy, Huxley speaks not only of the circulation of what he calls "primitive" texts, but also of his wish to develop those conditions everywhere that allow for the creation, circulation, and appreciation of the individual expressive geniuses who best represent their cultures. Recall that the Collection of Representative Works was originally designed not just to bring works into the dominant languages but also to sponsor the translation of all the world's best literature into many "lesser known" and less dominant tongues. Huxley writes that expecting "to be moved and enriched by Hamlet, or one of Beethoven's posthumous Quartets . . . without some preparatory effort . . . is like expecting a man with flabby untrained muscles . . . to derive immediate benefit from a twenty-five mile walk in the mountains."[21] He advocated the global spread of a modernized public education system, highlighting science in particular, to discipline all those flabby muscles. Culture would play a supporting role in helping people to reach the necessary standard, and their own cultural level would in turn be raised over the course of a comprehensive education.

It is hard not to see an apparent tension here. The translation of classic literature would help to establish intercultural communication, making the great classics available to what Huxley considered less developed cultures while making preindustrial arts available to those whose decadence needed to be checked. But the process of political, economic, cultural, and social modernization, the creation of a global archive of existing knowledge and thought, and the fostering of progress by harmonizing the cultures of the West and its others, threatened the very values of tradition, community, and localism that Huxley and his fellow cosmopolitans thought the West needed to respect if it hoped to correct the ravages of progress.

Huxley, however, did not apparently see this as much of a problem. Instead, he believed that a program like the Collection of Representative Works could offset precisely such worries. This was one of the ways in which cosmopolitan elites managed the concern that the sort of development promoted by UNESCO might threaten cultures not yet tainted by modernity: by offering those cultures the opportunity to preserve their monuments—monuments to times past and, soon, not so readily accessible—in a permanent archive of other tributes to what progress necessarily transcends.

* * *

And the program offered the former imperial powers even more. In their short treatise, *The Future of the Colonies*, Huxley and the historian Phyllis Deane write about how "the expansion of the white races" was changing its character by the

1940s. "Conquest, settlement and economic pillage can now have only a historical interest, as exhibits of past ages in the world's historical museum," they suggest. But this doesn't mean that global trade is finished or should proceed without the guidance of the former imperial powers.[22] Instead, Huxley and Deane impugn the earlier type of colonial expansion because it was based on the assumption that resources were scarce and must be expropriated and fought over. This mentality prevented humanity from embarking on an even more substantially expansive achievement: a "universal minimum standard and its progressive raising." They argue that "the only type of expansion that is now legitimate . . . is a cultural expansion," and the "cultural expansion" that they have in mind entails the former colonizers coming to terms with the fact that everyone has a right to the same standard of living and everyone can achieve it through an enlightened progressive policy.[23]

The Future of the Colonies advocates for something that Huxley often trumpeted, including in his role as UNESCO's director general: an enlightened, non-imperialist international community and a focus on attacking the worst poverty by raising living standards with the help of experts from the developed economies. In an earlier article, "Colonies and Freedom," Huxley articulates his vision of Britain's continued role in this ongoing progress as an expert and guide in the colonies. He argues that British colonialism must be placed within the larger history of what he calls "white capitalist expansion," defending Britain's continued involvement in the regions in which it has had colonial interests. Expansion occurred in the United States, too, he points out, though mainly internally, where it was "achieved by means of purchase, a war, and expropriation of the American Indians." His key point, though, is that this expansion now needed to concern itself not with physical barriers, internal or external, but rather with "the frontier of the standard of living," which is not about "the two-dimensional surface of the earth" but rather "a third dimension, of human welfare, in which expansion can continue indefinitely." The question of the fate of the colonies is really the much broader question of how to develop "backward areas." In Huxley's view, the "restrictionist tendencies of monopoly capitalism" are an impediment; his interest is in "launching world economics once more on the tide of expansionism."[24] For the accomplishment of this expansion, the crucial matter is not whether nations have national sovereignty but whether they have reached the right standard of development.

In the 1940s, Huxley himself traveled to West Africa to help with a project to develop local science education, and "Colonies and Freedom" was written in anticipation of the trip. Nor was this his first official involvement with colonial institutions and programs. In 1929, the British Colonial Office had sent him to British East Africa to report on how one might improve colonial education in biology.[25] He reported that "if contact with a bit of the British Colonial Empire has not yet made me a full-blooded devotee of kiplingismus it has certainly shown me the way to a spirit of Liberal Imperialism."[26] If progress in the "provision" of education had been slower than people might like, he argued, this was not because of any fault of the British imperial project. It was rather a reflection of what was required by the culture of the underdeveloped societies—those "flabby muscles." He stated that these societies had thus far existed in a state of "barbarism, without written language, the plow, the wheel, or stone building." Given such conditions, they simply could not "be provided with the intellectual (or material) equipment of the modern world in a few decades."[27]

Though Huxley was a controversial figure within UNESCO and his official reign only lasted a few years, his developmentalist ethos was considered common sense at the time. In 1946, Léon Blum, as president of UNESCO's First General Conference, advocated that the organization focus on eradicating illiteracy, asking: "How can UNESCO hope to operate satisfactorily in a world *more than half* of whose inhabitants cannot even read or write, and are without the basis of ideas upon which there can be built healthy living or prosperous agriculture, and in general any rational applications of science? . . . How can people lead the good life, and how can we expect them to bother about education, if they are undernourished and diseased?"[28] Blum, a three-time prime minister of France, defined himself as a socialist and believed that a progressive state managed by experts like himself was the best way to prevent poverty and war. Literacy, agricultural development, and rational science had to emerge in integral combination.

Huxley had applauded the 1940 British Colonial Development and Welfare Act as the manifestation of just such a progressive state, one that was willing to "enlarge" the British colonial project to include "social welfare, health and education." He singled out one of the act's first provisions, of money for the West African Institute of Arts, Industries and Social Sciences, deeming it "our first large-scale encouragement of secondary industry among the backward peoples. . . . Tiles, pottery and stoneware are already being manufactured locally to save shipping space and to meet the increasing military and civilian needs." Without British help in orchestrating such initiatives and training people to participate, the colonies would not achieve prosperity. In what he clearly conceived as a benevolent and conscientious view, he claimed that all of the people of the colonies, "not just the administration, or the intelligentsia and the chiefs, or the trading companies and foreign capital," should "be brought to realize that they can attain a new security and a new standard of living and health and interest, and that this is more worth while than the old."[29] And he wrote with Deane that

> the working man's standard of life depends on the accumulated knowledge, equipment, wealth and traditions of the society in which he lives. From this common stock he may draw the economic and social advantages which accrue from ports, roads, and drainage systems, the long life and good health which result from a national store of medical knowledge . . . the cultural pleasures to be derived from the national store of art treasures, educational institutions endowed with scholarly traditions and often supported by the wealth of past generations, and a form of social organization which satisfies some of the most urgent needs for self-expression.[30]

Huxley acknowledged that what he was envisioning was basically a project of total reeducation, which would require a series of capital investments. Public and private interests would have to be brought into it. Foreign capital would be essential, he argued, given "proper control," which means the "restriction of profits to a certain moderate percentage, with the compulsory plowing-back of anything above this into the colonial territories." Public expenditure would do its part supporting "roads, harbors, dams, power plants, warehouses and processing facilities, schools, hospitals and schemes of agricultural credit" so that the regions in question might finally be able to "make their economic contribution to the world."

We are cautioned not to think, then, in terms of an end to imperialism. Even if we grant (as does Huxley) that the latter has its "ugly aspects"—especially in its non-British variants—the goal is not to eradicate imperial rule but rather to transform it into social and economic trusteeship in the form of "a campaign for the all-around development of backward areas and backward peoples."[31] In fact, even the then-prevalent ideal of imperial trusteeship was something Huxley rejected, preferring to suggest that the new relationships be ones not of trusteeship but of partnership. We have already seen, though, that he was quick to specify that the standard of development would be the one evident in the already evolved economies and that aid to developing nations would necessarily come from white experts acting as guides.

The Future of the Colonies argues the point quite boldly:

> We the separate colonial powers and the white race as a whole, can and should still
> export brains and skill to the colonies, can and should help their people to acquire
> such of our ideas and inventions as will help their advance, can and should fertil-
> ize their countries with our accumulated wealth and our accumulated experience,
> and with the machines and techniques to which they have given rise. That will help
> the colonial peoples; but it will also help the economic prosperity of the world as a
> whole, including that of the colonial powers.[32]

In the *Yale Review*, Huxley continued the argument, writing that the backward
places were "to pass through [the developed world's] Renaissance, its Industrial
revolution, and its transition to the Age of Air Transport and the Social Service
State, all simultaneously." The white races, in a "next and final phase of white
expansion," were assigned the task of bringing about this crucial "development
of the world's backward and undeveloped regions, of which the colonies are an
important section."[33]

* * *

It would be foolish to separate UNESCO's Collection of Representative Works
from this activity of securing the former imperial powers' ongoing trusteeship
and dominant position in anchoring and orchestrating global development. The
program partook of the work of "cultural expansion" that intellectuals such as
Huxley envisioned as the accompaniment to the general advancement of progress
in human achievement. As a cultural program, it was meant to be a symbol of
human community and partnership across borders and to contribute to efforts
to create the conditions for collective social progress. The mark of true "progress"
would be the rectification of the fact that there were still societies around the
world that did not yet enjoy developed economies. Huxley's lament was, bluntly,
that not everyone was yet able to escape the poverty of communal life, and they
could thus not participate on equal terms, as free rights-bearing individuals, in a
globalizing economy, selling their labor, purchasing commodities, and developing
modern scientific, technical, and cultural wealth to share with others.

Sponsoring the translation of classic literature sounds perfectly laudable
and benign, of course, and no doubt its actual political role was a minor one. It
was, nevertheless, an activity that reflected the mentalities I have outlined here.
It shared in the faith that a fundamental and shattering transformation would

see the replacement of Europe's former empires, which had been premised on plunder and inequality, with a new kind of willing partnership defined by common goals and shared intellectual foundations. Supremacy would for the time being still belong to Europeans, but their ultimate interest would be in sharing the fruits of their wealth—sophisticated knowledge in science, engineering, agriculture, literature, and much else—with people with whom they claimed to seek an ultimate camaraderie and equality. The new prosperity of the formerly impoverished would then reverberate to the benefit of their enlightened white-race stewards in the form of political stability and increased trade.

The Collection of Representative Works was designed as a program of respectful cultural exchange among equals, part of building the foundations of the newly secure global polity. These ends were hardly politically neutral, as security was tied inexorably to modernization, and being modern meant living in a liberal capitalist society and, ideally, participating actively and equally, as workers and consumers, in the globalizing market economy. It is hardly surprising, then, to discover that white experts played dominant roles in the early years of the Collection of Representative Works—that it turned out to be largely an incorporative canon. The world's various literatures were absorbed into English and French, which were thereby solidified in their roles as the languages of expert adjudication of the merit of literary works from any region. An elite intercultural community had the Collection of Representative Works as an inducement and accompaniment to its evolution toward a higher state of consciousness and sympathetic community. Knowledge of the classic writings of all peoples evinced the respectful interest of the imperial "partner" in the underdeveloped regions that were the targets of programs to improve living standards. It guarded the developed world's acquisitive position in relation to the world's cultural wealth, gave the white races some enlivening exposure to the non-decadent and precapitalist holism that were expected to be found in the "lesser known" literatures, and preserved what might have otherwise disappeared with the inevitable and welcome further development of Huxley's vaunted capitalist expansion, orchestrated and controlled by white people.

* * *

As it happens, in 1947 a full 514 of the 557 UNESCO Secretariat posts were held by French or English nationals.[34] Yet race was a key topic in the organization's early days, and the nature of its discussion is revealing. In describing the first comprehensive statement on race (the "Statement on Race, Paris, July 1950"), which the

United Nations Economic and Social Council had asked UNESCO to devise in 1949, Vijay Prashad claims that what they came up with was to "transform the insistence on biological difference to an appreciation for cultural diversity."[35] This is true to a point and was an important development. Yet the original statement, which denied that there was any biological truth to the very concept of race, had to be modified after scientists, mainly British and American, complained about the preponderance of anthropologists weighing in. They insisted that there were in fact effective biological realities that informed individual behavior.[36]

Huxley himself had a very complex and carefully worked-out take on the matter of biological determinism. He took the evolution of organisms toward greater levels of individual autonomy and "wholeness" as the model proof that we could objectively measure progress. At the foundation of Huxley's scientific humanism was the belief that a verifiable doctrine of progress was the necessary foundation for feeling that one's life had purpose and direction. His biology was, in Roger Smith's terms, "an expressive vehicle for social values": "evolutionary theory underwrote belief in progress, providing authority for a world-view representing progress as natural." Images of "increase in individuality up the evolutionary scale" appeared to provide "a concrete criterion of progress applicable equally to nature and to society."[37] Huxley's observations about biological organisms were thus crucial to his conception of human development as a whole and to his view of culture's supporting role. Some individual organisms were inferior, not yet having developed their innate capacity for movement into their ideal individual wholeness. Marshalled wisely, culture could help them get there. The Collection of Representative Works was also then, in this respect, an "expressive vehicle for social values."

While Huxley abandoned some of his earlier and more extreme eugenicist positions after World War II—the belief that only superior individuals should be able to reproduce, for example—he never fully disavowed the core notion that "biology explains character, and that character, or the capacity for individuality, is both the key to social advance and an ethical ideal."[38] His 1935 book *We Europeans: A Survey of "Racial" Problems*, written with the Cambridge ethnologist A. C. Haddon, never suggests that biology is irrelevant to racial difference, and his subsequent statements on race do not depart much from that.[39] Nor was Huxley unusual. Michelle Brattain has exhaustively detailed the extent to which, despite UNESCO's stated goal of repudiating racist thought, most of its scientists "proved unwilling to question the validity of race as a natural category." UNESCO's second official statement on race ("Statement on the Nature of Race and Race Difference,

Paris, 1951"), produced after lively debate about the anti-biologism of the first statement, moved away from the earlier social constructivist emphasis to return, at least in part, to a biological definition, even going so far as to note "differences between 'non-literate' and 'more civilized' people on intelligence tests."[40]

Early UNESCO-backed works such as Juan Comas's *Racial Myths* (1952), Claude Lévi-Strauss's *Race and History* (1952), and Michel Leiris's *Race and Culture* (1952) do present race in fundamental relation to colonial and capitalist social formations and do suggest that these structuring realities would have to be transformed before racism could really be addressed.[41] But for the most part at UNESCO, when it came to official statements of organizational purview, racial bias was presented as simply outmoded and as something that UNESCO was well positioned to attack. The Collection of Representative Works was itself described as an engine of understanding across races, able to undermine biases by revealing common humanity. In other words, during this stage in UNESCO's history, race was not yet conceived as a means of arranging the maldistribution of resources, as later thinkers would have it. All that could be glimpsed was the opportunity for limitless growth toward a shared modernity and anti-racist enlightenment.

The fact that Huxley has often been described as an important anti-racist—despite his sense that with expert guidance from the "white race," humanity would evolve like a biological organism into the realization of its own suprahumanity—speaks to the nature of the analysis of race that was palatable at the time. There were clearly superior and inferior races in Huxley's schema; it was only through close guidance by the superior that the inferior could be brought up to the same level. If there was any inequity in the distribution of resources and standards of living, this would be righted through the sound management of new educational systems, cultural uplift, direct foreign investment, and public support for infrastructure projects.

Thus, in Glenda Sluga's terms, UNESCO's projects at this time, including the seemingly innocuous work of translating the world's classic literature via the Collection of Representative Works, signal "the ways in which late nineteenth-century conceptions of race and empire remained uneasily at the heart of cosmopolitanism and internationalism."[42] With UNESCO's help, development, in the form of an "imperially directed political and economic modernization," became "a new anchor of imperial legitimacy."[43]

2 America's Postwar Hegemony

THE JAPANESE SERIES within the Collection of Representative Works, which eventually extended to a few dozen titles, released its first translation into English in 1956. The fact that there was a Japanese Series within the Collection of Representative Works in the first place was a coup for the Japanese national commission to UNESCO. The Japanese government had promoted the nation's literary riches through the Society for International Cultural Relations since the 1930s. In the postwar period, when Japan sought to secure its reputation as a cultured, Western-facing, peace-loving democracy, it was hard to find a better medium for that than UNESCO, which was an international symbol of commitment to peaceful coexistence and mutual respect.

Yasunari Kawabata's oeuvre was crucial to this undertaking. His global reputation was secured in 1956, when *Snow Country*, originally published in 1937 as *Yukiguni*, was translated into English under the auspices of the Collection of Representative Works and published in the United States by Alfred A. Knopf. Knopf's editor-in-chief at the time, Harold Strauss, oversaw a significant publishing program for Japanese literature in English translation in the United States—thirty-four Knopf titles between 1955 and 1977, including a handful backed by the Collection of Representative Works.

UNESCO often took recommendations from PEN International and from regional PEN branches about which works to translate. As a promoter of translation, and with many PEN members themselves working as translators, PEN had a natural interest in the health of the Collection of Representative Works. Kawabata was president of the Japanese branch of PEN from 1948 to 1965, a role in which he championed the translation of Japanese literature, including, not infrequently, his own work. Strauss had become aware of Kawabata and became interested in *Snow Country* just as Kawabata was himself arranging for its publication via the UNESCO translation program. Strauss subsequently came to an agreement with

UNESCO, stipulating that Knopf would bear the costs that arose from publication of the translation, while UNESCO would purchase two hundred copies of the book and help promote it via its many publications.

Strauss had become interested in Japanese literature after having been unexpectedly assigned to study Japanese as part of the Army Languages program during the war. He then spent ten months in postwar Japan, serving the US occupation as a print media monitor. He was surprised to discover that Japan had a thriving literary culture. When he returned to his job at Knopf, he sought out Japanese works for a program that would complement the press's established reputation as a translator of European literature. He anticipated significant funding from relevant outside sources. While traveling in Tokyo in 1952, he wrote to Knopf that he had "arranged for a very substantial amount of Rockefeller money (John D., III) to be made available to finance translations from Japanese into English, beginning in March, 1953. . . . This is being done through Shigeharu Matsumoto, a most important man in Japan, and the managing director of International House, an organization already set up for just such projects (cultural interchange) with Rockefeller and other money."[1] Other private foundation money found its way into Japanese translations as well. The Ford Foundation funded training for translators by awarding fellowships that stationed them in Japan. The translator of *Snow Country*, Edward Seidensticker, had himself been a Ford Foundation fellow before going on to translate dozens of works of Japanese literature into English.

Snow Country was the first and most enduringly famous novel by Kawabata included in the UNESCO program. In 1968, when Kawabata became the first Japanese writer to win the Nobel Prize for Literature, it was mentioned as one of the works that the prize committee was especially eager to commend. The first edition featured on its cover an image of a geisha, eyes downcast, against a snowy backdrop, and the book was generally marketed as a deeply Japanese story, marked by a pervasive and fatalistic sadness, that highlighted enduring cultural traditions. Since that review, Kawabata's writing has often been commended for its lyricism and its preservation of traditional, even ancient beauty, and his oeuvre has been in part responsible for the formation of what Miho Matsugu calls "a dominant world image of Japan."[2] In awarding him his Nobel Prize, the Swedish committee praised him for his "clear tendency to cherish and preserve a genuinely national tradition" and for having captured "the essence of the Japanese mind." In his work, they state, "it is still possible to find a sensitively shaded situation poetry which traces its origin back to Murasaki's vast canvas of life and manners in Japan about the year 1000."[3]

At the same time, the 1956 English translation of *Snow Country* is a quint-essential piece of Cold War culture and of American economic and cultural hegemony. It tapped into the postwar vogue for anti-political writing—writing that positioned its own insight into individual perspectives against any kind of purportedly reductive systemic thinking. At the time, many mainstream US literary writers and critics stressed the value of the literary as an expression of personal experience in resistance to totalitarianism, communism, and "group think." More than that, they maintained that literature at its best could only be evidence of the superior value of the individual's inner life, understood as au-tomatically autonomous and impervious and never determined by any outside forces of ideology or state.[4]

The Cold War climate thus found writers and critics repudiating what Henry Schwartz describes as "the socially conscious literary traditions of naturalism/realism," preferring instead "an elitist aesthetic—an aesthetic that claimed im-portant literature was remote, complex, iconoclastic, and inaccessible, and re-quired interpretation."[5] Kawabata's established position in the Japanese literary field made him perfectly suited for the move into his new international role as a champion of this aesthetic. A premiere member of a self-conscious school of lyrical writers, Kawabata deliberately disavowed the proletarian commitments that had been in vogue during his university days in the 1920s as a student of English and Japanese literature. He was vocal about his faith in the fundamental separation of art from the political sphere, in love with abstruse symbolism, and actively aligned with American writers who shared his tendencies.

In 1955, when Strauss helped to arrange a visit to Japan by William Faulkner as part of his efforts to market and develop Knopf's Japanese translations, he wrote to Kawabata asking that he entertain Faulkner during the trip. Faulkner was traveling under the official auspices of the Exchange of Persons Branch of the United States Information Service and was to give a number of talks, including one at the an-nual American literature seminar that the US government sponsored for Japanese teachers of English.[6] Faulkner was able to act as a representative of the American state—in theory, at least, though in fact he was debilitatingly drunk throughout much of the trip—because of his central role in the repudiation of more socially oriented literary modes associated with communism, totalitarianism, group think, and censorship. And though Kawabata's *Snow Country* was written largely in the 1930s, while Japan was at war, with one final sequence added during the US oc-cupation of Japan after World War II, it is akin to Faulkner's work in its deliberate avoidance of any position-taking on the politically immediate. The novel is instead grounded in what Sidney Devere Brown describes as a "private world of beauty and culture" that "eschews [direct] commentary on social and political problems."[7] When other literature and the arts were being drawn into Cold War cultural diplomacy campaigns, treated as emblems of "the freedom of the individual under capitalism" and as testaments to "the plight of man in the modern world," *Snow Country* was given as evidence of the universality of the grounding of literary art in individual psychic life and integral personal freedom.[8]

The novel's compatibility with the vogue in US literature of that time for apolitical lyricism also made it suitable for inclusion in UNESCO's Collection of Representative Works. In the program's first decades, its sentimental globalism, based on the premise that war and prejudice could be overcome through respect for diversity and recognition of affinities, complemented and reinforced American aims for the United States to become a lodestar for world affairs. The idea of American centrality was partly justified on the grounds that America's leaders valued intercultural understanding and had faith in the integral unity and similarity of human experience across borders. As Arthur Schlesinger Jr. wrote in *The Vital Center*, which was to become a popular manifesto for a "new liberalism":

> The individual requires a social context, not one imposed by coercion, but one freely emerging in response to his own needs and initiatives. Industrialism has inflicted savage wounds on the human sensibility; the cuts and gashes are to be healed only by a conviction of trust and solidarity with other human beings. . . . We require individualism which does not wall man off from community; we require community which sustains but does not suffocate the individual.[9]

Because industrialization and urbanization threatened the communal ties of traditional societies, and because these were then replaced only with fragmentation, blight, anomie, alienation, and anxiety, people experienced as a burden what purported to be liberation from communal obligations. There was, then, a profound need to foster awareness of and respect for social bonds of community and relationality.

Totalitarianism, especially manifest in Soviet communism, was the bad answer to the question of how to alleviate the burden of excessive personal freedom, restore the bonds of community, and provide a compelling respite to the prevailing anomie. As Schlesinger wrote:

Who can live without desperation in a society turned asocial—in a social system which represents organized frustration instead of organized fulfillment? Freedom has lost its foundation in community and become a torment; "individualism" strips the individual of layer after layer of protective tissue. Reduced to panic, industrial man joins the lemming migration, the convulsive mass escape from freedom to totalitarianism, hurling himself from the bleak and rocky cliffs into the deep, womb-dark sea below.[10]

As the new vital center of world affairs, the United States needed to foster a genuine world community across societies defined not by control but by consent—societies of free assent to liberal democracy, free enterprise, and tolerance that leaned "toward compromise, persuasion and consent in politics, toward tolerance and diversity in society."[11] It is hard not to notice here the striking echoes of Julian Huxley's visions of postimperial partnership and of living standards endlessly rising.

To be clear, my suggestion is not that Kawabata as a private individual was wholly supportive of the project of establishing the United States as the world's new vital center. It is rather that UNESCO's Collection of Representative Works was part of the postwar activity of forging bonds of mutual respect across borders and of creating a global community of sympathetic intellectuals. Kawabata's overall literary project was compatible with this activity; the fact that he does not comment directly on war or occupation is part of that compatibility. His interest in using his work to preserve Japanese folk traditions, explored further below, is part of it as well. Even when his work tends toward lamenting what is lost in the drive toward modernization—and his later novels are quite critical of Western threats to Japanese traditions—this does not make it incompatible with the United States' new liberal internationalism, which was conscientious about precisely such loss and respectfully interested in outmoded traditions. The new liberal internationalism and humanism, enshrined perhaps above all in the United Nations' 1948 Declaration of Human Rights, were precisely directed against the old modes of unthinking domination and cultural erasure. Instead, the preference was to imagine a new international order built on mutual respect, individual rights, and a shared desire to preserve monuments to authentic human diversity.

Kawabata's extensive work with PEN at the time, as well as PEN's status as official adviser to UNESCO, are telling in this respect. As part of his long tenure as president of PEN's Japanese chapter, Kawabata oversaw the organization's twenty-ninth international congress, held in Tokyo in 1957—the first-ever PEN congress held in the Far East. As the president of a national PEN branch, he was in frequent communication with UNESCO. PEN for its part consistently backed what Megan Doherty has described as a liberal, humanistic, and "aesthetically middlebrow" approach to literature and its possible social roles. In the immediate postwar period, PEN worked to turn such values as support for artistic freedom and individual self-expression into universal truths. It attracted funding from foundations and governments during the Cold War on this basis, as part of the ongoing project of helping to "make liberal humanism seem synonymous with internationalism"[12]—and, I would add, of making both liberal humanism and internationalism synonymous with good literature.

UNESCO, PEN, the US intellectual establishment, and Kawabata were thus all united in the overarching ideological project of enshrining liberal humanist internationalism as the official culture of the US-based development era—a fitting prop for the idealization of liberal capitalist democracy as the only conduit to genuine progress and liberty, as the best means of securing those human rights that the United Nations had just encoded. Naturally, literature affiliated with this project had to be broadly sympathetic to and compatible with its goals.

* * *

The formal US cultural policy establishment was beginning to solidify during this same period. As part of that process, American support for culture and the arts became more extensive, linking cultural funding to international diplomacy and to democratic public life because there was money available for that and because it could be assigned a role in securing US dominance in the Cold War.[13] In a 1953 speech, Walter Laves, the chair of the US national commission to UNESCO, stated that

> in our lifetime we have left behind the epoch in which large portions of mankind had the status of dependence on Western powers. . . . Economic subordination is being rejected, along with political. They cast off the role of mere suppliers of raw materials to the factories of the West. They seek to advance with giant strides from the low levels of mere subsistence and semistarvation. This is the fundamental revolution of our age.[14]

The goal of his speech was to explain why American financial support for UNESCO was such a strategically sound idea. He was speaking to a meeting of businesspeople, and in the pamphlet publication of the talk, he is pictured standing next to Harry A. Bullis, then chair of the board of General Mills, Inc.

Bullis was also chairing the conference at which Laves spoke, which was dedicated to the topic of "America's Stake in International Cooperation."

UNESCO was, in Laves's estimation, simply good value for money, given that the United States was at the time contributing a mere $3 million to UNESCO's budget, one third of the organization's annual country-funded budget ($9 million from a total of 60 countries); an additional $3 million came from the United Nations Fund for Economic Development, giving UNESCO a total annual budget of $12 million. Laves notes approvingly that the UN development fund was similar to the Point Four Program, in that both were designed to "furnish technical assistance to underdeveloped countries."[15] He writes that "We need markets overseas and opportunities for investment. There is nothing to be ashamed of in this. A country can get wealthy by conquest and exploitation, or it can get wealthy by production and trade. We have a right to be proud that the United States has always chosen the course of production and trade." He further explains how support for the economic development of distant nations is a way to create new consumers for American products. Comparing Pakistan and Sweden, he notes that Pakistan, "economically impoverished, rural, unindustrialized," imports from the United States what amounts to a value of $0.50 per person, while Sweden, "highly developed with a prosperous industry," imports $16.20 worth per person. On the list he provides of things plaguing the less-developed nations—"semistarvation, pestilence, endemic disease"—he includes "low consumption of energy," illiteracy, and "a minimum of participation in world trade." It is for these reasons, he argues, that the United States must subsidize economic development by contributing to UNESCO: not only in support of distant people's natural aspirations to achieve American-style modernity—with improved levels of literacy, energy use, and global trade capacity—but "for the maintenance and enrichment of the American economy."[16]

And so, with such ends in view, the United States expanded its postwar global power and Americans spread out around the world—students, translators, corporate executives, social scientists, and the like. The American occupation of Japan was one of the first major postwar projects of this kind. US forces worked to prevent Japan from falling prey to Soviet influence. They promoted democracy and helped to restore the industries destroyed by the war, while new peace and security treaties granted them extensive military rights and provided the foundation for de facto power that lasted for decades.[17] It was with this expansion of US global hegemony in places like Japan that there arose a new liberal internationalism and what Christina Klein describes as a new "global imaginary based on connection."[18]

A January 1955 special issue of *The Atlantic* included a 78-page supplement, "Perspective of Japan." Akira Kurosawa's *Rashomon* was screened at the 1955 Venice Film Festival, where it was highly celebrated. Harold Strauss published his own fiction set in Japan in *The New Yorker*—a story called "Ayame," based on his encounter with a Tokyo nightclub hostess.[19] He also published numerous articles in *The Atlantic*, *Publishers Weekly*, and other prominent outlets about the delights of Japanese literature and the value of intercultural exchange. In a 1954 article discussing his work to develop a series of English translations, Strauss writes: "All the people who have given me such unstinting help seem to feel that in such a close association in practical affairs we cannot afford to remain ignorant of the true feelings and inner emotional life of the Japanese." He remarks further that it is "the novel, for all its present troubles," that still provides "the best means of communicating feelings."[20] Seidensticker, the translator of *Snow Country*, was one of the two best-known American translators of Japanese literature. The other was Donald Keene. Both worked with prominent New York publishers; both worked closely with Kawabata and accompanied him to the Nobel Prize ceremony as interpreters; and both—like Harold Strauss—had learned part of their Japanese from the US Army Languages program.

Klein argues that throughout the 1950s, the proliferating depictions of Asia tended to express the ideals of reciprocity, of sentimental bonds forged by solidarities, of mutual exchange and benefit, and of "the possibility of transcending particularity by recognizing a common and shared humanity." There arose, especially, what she describes as "narratives of anti-conquest."[21] *Snow Country* can be read in this light. It imagines a reciprocal love that the protagonist, Shimamura, is incapable of achieving. The geisha Komako insists that she is not required to do anything for men and that intimacy is a matter of her own choosing. It is an image of the geisha as motivated by affection and desire for human intimacy, rather than by coercion. The possibility of true human congress is thematized in *Snow Country* within this ideal of romantic intimacy. The promise of authentic contact and communication, which grounds the sentimental globalism of both the Collection of Representative Works and America's "new liberalism," has a substantial presence in the novel, as an ideal that Shimamura himself fails to live up to.

Klein's interpretation remains persuasive. The sentimental education provided by works like *Snow Country* was part of creating the conditions for the
acceptance of a new global economic order with America in the dominant role.
This was to be an order based not on oppression or coercion but on something
that would be far more appealing to developing nations otherwise tantalized by
involvement with the Soviets: a "partnership," featuring commitments, responsibilities, and obligations to what a widely attended Museum of Modern Art
exhibition called "The Family of Man." This exhibition toured all over the world
under the auspices of the United States Information Agency, including in Japan,
and was visited by some nine million people.

* * *

Snow Country, which was published in the United States in the wake of the formal
US occupation of and ongoing de facto control over Japan, and during a time of
heightened efforts to support and justify American worldmaking, is the story of
a man who thwarts the ideal of respectful romance; with its emphasis on private
feeling, personal relationships, and lyrical descriptions of the snowbound coun-
tryside, it was ideally suited for worldwide elite literary appreciation.

The novel aestheticizes rather than politicizes its figures. Militarism and nation-
making are deliberately left out of the picture. Shimamura is a wealthy, leisured
dilettante who experiences the standard anomie and boredom of city life and
seeks relief in the company of a hot-springs geisha, Komako. His wife and children
remain in Tokyo and are only glimpsed. His intimate relationships are always mediated, never complete, and he himself is dimly aware that he lacks some essential
feeling that his lover Komako is able to achieve. Komako is, we gather, meant to
be little more than a tragic symbol of inevitable decay—decay both of her own
sensual beauty and of an imperial Japan eroded by modernization.

In the introduction to his 1956 translation, Seidensticker contrasts Komako, the hot-springs geisha, with her counterparts in Tokyo. She is nearly a
social outcast; her pretense to being an artist of any kind is very thin. She is
more clearly a prostitute and so, he writes, "a particularly poignant symbol of
wasted, decaying beauty."[22] Shimamura is depicted as needing to think of her
in his own way, fatalistically, as a symbol first and foremost of human frailty.
He needs his experiences with her to be mediated by symbolism. The novel's
famous opening lines highlight his inability to look directly at a woman, Yoko,
on the train. He prefers to focus on her reflection in the glass and is taken with

the way her visage becomes indistinguishable from the landscape they are passing. Her ministrations to the sick man traveling with her—he turns out to have once been involved romantically with Komako, and she works in part to pay his medical bills—are not sad to Shimamura, nor painful. It is, rather, "as if he were watching a tableau in a dream—and that was no doubt the working of his strange mirror" (9).

Shimamura has lately been translating "French treatises on the dance from the golden age of the Russian ballet," and is pleased to be associated with literary people in part because of their connections to Western aesthetic traditions. His interest in "the western dance" is described as "more than simple fascination with the exotic and the unknown" (24–25), because mediation is crucial to his experience of it. The very distance of it from his own cultural experience is a source of interest for him: "The pleasure he found in his new hobby came in fact from his inability to see with his own eyes westerners in western ballets." He knows them only from study, not from having been in attendance at any. Shimamura's appreciation for Western ballet, and later, we see, his love for Japanese folk traditions, both fall into this category: they are things that he can especially romanticize precisely because he's never witnessed them in an immediate way. We read that

> a ballet he had never seen was an art in another world. It was an unrivalled armchair reverie, a lyric from some paradise. He called his work research, but it was actually free, uncontrolled fantasy. He preferred not to savor the ballet in the flesh; rather he savored the phantasms of his own dancing imagination, called up by Western books and pictures. It was like being in love with someone he had never seen. (25)

Furthermore, as we have already begun to suspect, it is "possible that, hardly knowing it, he was treating the woman exactly as he treated the western dance" (25). He can be involved with women to the extent that he can insert some mediating force between him and them. In the case of Yoko, he holds her at a distance established in the opening scene on the train, where he looks at her reflection in the window of the train. Meanwhile, Komako, in her remote outpost, is easy to treat as a symbol of declining beauty and ardent service. Seeing her from the train window the first time he leaves her behind, he thinks, "it was as though one strange piece of fruit had been left behind in the grimy glass case of a shabby mountain grocery" (85). She herself reflects, "I could go pleasantly to seed here in the mountains. It would be a fine, quiet feeling" (142).

But why, one wonders, is it easy to depict a figure like Komako as trapped in her role as a hot-springs geisha? What is behind the surface symbolism of her devotion to Shimamura, and the fact that it seems clear that she cannot leave this remote outpost and has little hope of starting on a path toward other life pursuits? Miho Matsugu has described how geisha were often used as supports for empire-building, including when Japan invaded Manchuria in 1931, and then Shanghai in 1932, before the war with China began in 1937. The government made money from the licensing fees that the geisha and their houses paid, and businesses served by the geisha brought money into local economies. The military also depended on the services of the geisha to boost soldiers' morale. While stationed in China, the military recruited women to cater to soldiers' needs in notorious "comfort" stations, where their overt Japaneseness—in hair, dress, makeup, and artistry—was especially prized. They were "deployed as figures of cultural authenticity" and supports to nationalist militarism.[23]

The economic realities of sex work in Japan in the 1930s were more complex even than this, however. Shimamura travels by train, where reflections in the windows enable his half-erotic reveries, but tax increases to fund the waging of war and other modernizing nation-building projects such as the railways had made subsistence farming and other traditional practices even more vulnerable than they already were. Many had to give up their farms altogether and move to the cities, and impoverished families were now more inclined to sell their daughters into prostitution or geisha work or to conclude that such work was better than no work at all. Hence, Matsugu writes, "geisha were a by-product of the imperialist endeavor, as well as a resource for it." Even as they were held up as symbols of traditional beauty and Japanese cultural authenticity, they were "contributing to the project of modernization: capitalist development, militarist expansion, and empire-building."[24]

The hot-springs geisha could exist out of view, too, whereas the urban geisha could not. The war efforts of the 1930s meant that women faced pressure to devote themselves to reproduction and to factory work, and there was a turn against open prostitution as representing a threat to traditional Japanese values. The image of the geisha was therefore desexualized and aestheticized, while explicit sex work was forbidden by laws like the Mother and Child Protection Law (1937) and the National Eugenics Law (1940).[25] The fact that Komako seems so trapped—that she cannot be a city geisha, cannot accompany Shimamura to Tokyo, cannot do anything but what she is already doing—is newly poignant when we consider the pressures sex workers faced during wartime: to work in direct service to the military forces, to disguise the sexual aspect of their service, or simply to hide in leisure centers like the hot-springs resort.

In this way, and despite what Kawabata's designs might have been, Komako's character is evidence of the way young girls were pushed into sex work in response to the Japanese militaristic imperialism and capitalist development of the 1930s. Even as Komako is held up as a symbol of beauty and its inevitable decay, and thus as a national icon for those who—like Shimamura, the elite male critic who idealizes traditional culture—seek cultural identification with a decadent regal imperium, she is a product of modernization, who learns to play her shamisen from sheet music and the radio. Kawabata based her character on a real geisha, Kodaka Kiku (1915–1999), one of ten children of a blacksmith, who was sent to become a geisha at age nine.[26] Kodaka's work was policed and regulated, and her prostitution was often a source of shame and hidden from view under the disguise of the authentic allure of the Japanese geisha. There is no absence of national political and military conscription in the novel, then. It is just buried in symbolism, and the conditions that made women like Komako into geisha are not explicitly mentioned, as they might have been in the proletarian literature that Kawabata disavowed. Kawabata instead participates in the transformation of the geisha into an icon of authentic Japaneseness that survives despite its own artificiality—despite radios and sheet music and imperialist wars and capitalist development.

It is precisely this transformation that makes his work available for conscription into UNESCO programming and the agenda of the US literary establishment of the time. The novel's doomed love affair even becomes the setting for a disquisition on the threatened clothmaking craft of Chijimi, whose market towns Shimamura visits by train in a fit of touristic fervor: "All of the Chijimi market towns had railway stations, and the region was still a well-known weaving center" (153). In a classic instance of elite fetishization of skilled craft labor—the same fetishization that is on display in Shimamura's respect for Komako's devotion—the tediousness of the clothmaking is what Shimamura admires most: "The thread was spun in the snow, and cloth woven in the snow, washed in the snow, and bleached in the snow." It was "the handwork of the mountain maiden through the long, snowbound winters." It has to be the hands of maidens, for "as they grew older they lost the touch that gave tone to the finest Chijimi. In their desire to be numbered among the few outstanding weavers, they put their whole labor and love into this product of the long snowbound months—the months of seclusion and boredom" (151). As in the case of the Western ballet, and the geisha, Shimamura is a connoisseur. He "searched for the cloth in the old-clothes shops" (150) and "had a standing order that when a good piece of Chijimi came in he was to see it" (151).

Seidensticker's introduction states that the novel depicts "life divorced from time through the long snowbound months" (vi). Yet as we have seen, the novel hardly lacks signs of modernity. It opens with the famous scene of Shimamura's travel by train to the hot springs. There is mention of avalanches and the risk of tunnels closing in and train stations being buried. Shimamura comforts himself with thoughts of snowplows and an electric avalanche warning system, its "five thousand workers . . . ready to clear away the snow, and two thousand young men from the volunteer fire-departments could be mobilized if they were needed" (6). These are, in fact, the necessary foundations of Shimamura's romantic pastoral. He insists on authentic Japanese traditional methods precisely because he lives the life of a modern Tokyo intellectual: "he wanted the bleaching to be done properly in the country where the maidens had lived." It is frustrating to him that, because "a Tokyo shop took care of the details for him . . . he had no way of knowing that the bleaching had really been done in the old manner" (152). His distance from the process enables his fascination but is also a source of consternation. It is clearly the fact that he does not himself work that makes his interest take the form that it does. He remarks that Komako, who is always working, is "hardly the person to ask about the fate of an old folk art" (153).

Lamenting that his love affair with Komako "would leave behind it nothing so definite as a piece of Chijimi" (154), "he began to wonder what was lacking in him, what kept him from living as completely" (155). The cloth is a stable icon; his relationship with Komako is a temporary fancy. The cloth is the product of centuries of tradition and seasons of patient effort; his relationship with Komako is just a distraction. Komako herself will "go to seed" in the mountains; the Chijimi cloth and the industry of appreciation surrounding it will last much longer, a stable marker and bastion of tradition against the perils of rapid transformation. The narrator, close to Shimamura's point of view, reflects

> that the weaver maidens, giving themselves to their work here under the snow, had lived lives far from as bright and fresh as the Chijimi they made. . . . In harsh economic terms the making of Chijimi was quite impractical, so great was the expenditure of effort that went into even one piece. It followed that none of the Chijimi

houses had been able to hire weavers from outside. The nameless workers, so diligent while they lived, had presently died, and only the Chijimi remained, the plaything of men like Shimamura. (157)

The sad fact being observed here is basically this: glory fades. What was once a respected tradition is now a "plaything." However, Shimamura himself is not impugned. His fascination with Chijimi cloth, and his ignorance of how the threat posed to it by capitalist industrialization is in fact the same threat posed to the families of women like Komako, are not derided. Capitalist development both threatens the traditional ways of making Chijimi cloth and makes Komako into a geisha, but it is only the first repercussion that seems worthy of Shimamura's extended lament.

"The labor into which a heart has poured its whole love—where will it have its say, to excite and inspire, and when?" (157), he asks. Here the remarkable appropriateness of the novel for inclusion in a UNESCO program is perfectly clear. The labor preserved in the cloth will "have its say," and excite and inspire, because agencies like UNESCO exist to preserve this particular novelistic vision of the tradition's importance, and then to preserve in turn examples of the folk art itself, specimens of the cloth in Japanese museums, where folk traditions emerge as a counterforce against the industrial factory.

Snow Country registers Japan's industrial strength and integration into global circuits only in its depiction of its protagonist's urban malaise and obsession with being witness to authentic culture. The novel is invested in the preservation of Japanese traditions in its own lyrical descriptions of valued craftwork. It is drawn also to study the nature of that interest itself, to understand the psychic comportment and relative leisure of those with the time and income to support cultural traditions in the name of aesthetic ideals. The novel's engagement with modernity is in other words mainly evident in its treatment of the psychic life of Shimamura: his startling anomie and alienation and his fascination with cultural traditions he understands as serving as fetishes for him precisely because they are in essence foreign to him. This is true both of his passion for the Western ballets he has never seen and of his interest in the making of Chijimi cloth in the remote Japanese winter—a process and product that he admires and covets as a connoisseur even as he acknowledges that he may have no way of knowing if he has ever seen the real thing.

This kind of investment in the preservation of folkways means that the novel anticipates UNESCO's later cultural programming, such as its insistence that cultural diversity can be respectfully maintained through the preservation of tangible and intangible heritage, and its development of resources such as lists of world heritage sites. At the time of its selection, the novel obviously fit into the Collection of Representative Works, because it embodied something evidently and definitively local to Japan, because it could serve as an emblem of Japanese culture for English-language readers. Likewise, it could also be leveraged by the Japanese branch of PEN because of its fundamental compatibility with liberal humanism, as a novel noncombatively interested in interiority and abstract symbolism. It was of interest in the United States because it was evidently literary in ways that made sense at the time, and because support for Japanese literature was itself meant to display US interest not just in occupation or domination but in cultural understanding and international community. By registering personal anomie and disavowing more politicized modes that might, for instance, impugn the Japanese imperium or the depredations of gender and social class, the novel makes itself available for conscription into a broader cultural transformation under US hegemony. This transformation of course entails the spreading of the same modernizing currents that undergird Shimamura's Chijimi fetish.

* * *

Objects, monuments, and practices that counter mass production remained integral to Kawabata's literary project throughout his career. *A Thousand Cranes* (1949–1951), written during the US occupation, focuses in part on the traditional tea ceremony and its commercialization. *The Old Capital* (1961–1962) is about Kyoto, "the home of artistic craft goods," and Kawabata wrote it in part because he "wanted to set down the beauty of the old city, Japan's capital from 794 to 1868, before it disappeared forever."[27] It focuses among other things on the obi, or kimono sash, which is meant to be bespoke, as a reflection of the wearer's personality. The novel glimpses the industrialization that has threatened the obi's traditional function, and construes the new giant factory that makes five hundred obi every day as an outside imposition, as "Western." Sidney Devere Brown describes Kawabata as a writer profoundly worried about the decline of the "old culture"—"a cultural nationalist who sought to preserve the world of tradition in novels before those traditions vanished forever."[28] The Nobel Prize committee made special note of this aspect of his work as well. It highlighted *The Old Capital* in particular, in a passage worth quoting at length:

The city itself is really the leading character, the capital of the old kingdom, once the seat of the mikado and his court, still a romantic sanctuary after a thousand years, the home of the fine arts and elegant handicraft, nowadays exploited by tourism but still a beloved place of pilgrimage. With its Shinto and Buddha temples, its old artisan quarters and botanical gardens, the place possesses a poetry that Kawabata expresses in a tender, courteous manner, with no sentimental overtones but, naturally, as a moving appeal. He has experienced his country's crushing defeat and no doubt realizes what the future demands in the way of industrial go-ahead spirit, tempo and vitality. But in the postwar wave of violent Americanization, his novel is a gentle reminder of the necessity of trying to save something of the old Japan's beauty and individuality for the new. He describes the religious ceremonies in Kyoto with the same meticulous care as he does the textile trade's choice of patterns in the traditional sashes belonging to the women's dresses. These aspects of the novel may have their documentary worth, but the reader prefers to dwell on such a deeply characteristic passage as when the party of middle-class people from the city visits the botanical garden—which has been closed for a long time because the American occupation troops have had their barracks there—in order to see whether the lovely avenue of camphor trees is still intact and able to delight the connoisseur's eye.[29]

And so, by the late 1960s, in the age of the counterculture and the Vietnam War, of emerging economic turbulence and crises of state legitimacy, what was deemed especially remarkable in Kawabata's work was how it charted the plight of a non-Western country whose traditions were being threatened by America's ongoing political and cultural influence. The specter of Americanization had by that time become a signal focus of Kawabata's work and its appreciation—as though there were some fundamental dissonance between capitalist industrialization and Japanese nationhood! Several of Kawabata's novels establish their claim to literariness by maligning the US presence in Japan and the industrialization of traditional practices. This is classic cultural nationalism, disposed not against capitalism and human immiseration in the service of wealth and nation, but against the American cultural imperialism that threatens cultural particularity. The capitalist engine of modernization is not itself a problem, so long as traditional Japanese practices are not threatened. This kind of cultural nationalism makes its claim on our attention on the grounds of its contribution to preserving things that might otherwise pass out of collective memory. UNESCO's programming from the late 1960s on, which is the focus of the next two chapters, had related emphases. Preserving folk traditions against the worst threats posed by the dominance of the hyper-developed economies, especially the United States, became a focus of UNESCO policy makers, and debates turned to the necessity of creating policies that would humanize a capitalism otherwise running rampant.

While *Snow Country* is addressed to an earlier moment, before Americanization had become such a consistent target of cultural scorn and before the crises plaguing the legitimacy of US dominance had begun to set in, Kawabata's cultural nationalism is already unmistakable. Workers like Komako and the "maiden" Chijimi makers possess a dignity that is associated with the mastery of craft, with ancient beauty, and with cultural tradition. As the novel that made Kawabata's literary reputation, *Snow Country* circulated within the literary world precisely because it refused to impugn US or Japanese militarist and capitalist modernization, preferring instead to memorialize the dignity of those who "serve" the nation. In this respect it accorded perfectly with the turn in the English-language literary sphere toward universal themes, the examination of psychic states, and the emphasis on individual particularity, psychology, interiority, and nuance, while offering to UNESCO the pleasing possibility of preserving some of the crucial symbols, icons, and practices of a particular culture—shamisen playing, Chijimi clothmaking, and the geisha. While the novel certainly understands the preservation of folk traditions as an elite project that stems from a desire to offset worries about modernization and to address a certain personal ennui, it simply notices, rather than criticizing, Shimamura's tendencies in this area. The novel became available as support for a forceful international liberal humanism for this reason. At bottom, the protagonist's personal romantic failures set up the mutuality of intimacy and accord as an alternative ideal, one that was broadly supported in US-backed narratives of anti-conquest popular at the time. Within the logic of the novel, Shimamura's fetishistic passion for Japanese folklife appears to be less of a problem. It is simply, rather, the natural inclination and activity of members of a cultural elite who are interested in preserving and respecting the integrity of human diversity.

In 2009, the making of Chijimi cloth was added to UNESCO's Representative List of the Intangible Cultural Heritage of Humanity.

3. Cultural Policy and the Perils of Development

A NUMBER OF STATE-BASED CULTURAL AGENCIES began to form in the postwar period—the Arts Council of Great Britain in 1946, the Canada Council for the Arts in 1957, and the French Ministry of Culture in 1959, to name only the most familiar. But an expert panel that UNESCO gathered in 1967, including among others Pierre Bourdieu, Mulk Raj Anand, Ousmane Sembène, and Richard Hoggart, offered the first official definition of cultural policy and inaugurated UNESCO's appeals to governments around the world to attend to the structure of their cultural institutions and funding apparatuses. Cultural policy, they stated, is "the sum total of the conscious and deliberate usages, action or lack of action in a society, aimed at meeting certain cultural needs through the optimum utilization of all the physical and human resources available to that society at a given time."[1] What would count as optimum utilization? Given all the needs of any society, how many resources could really be devoted to cultural pursuits? Could lack of action actually be counted as a form of policy provision? The statement, frustratingly vague, left much room for debate.

And debate was extensive. The report on the 1967 Paris proceedings was the first title in a new cultural policy book series, and the meeting itself was billed as preparation for the first official cultural policy roundtable, to be held in Monaco later that year. Many more meetings followed, covering cultural policy in Europe, Asia, Africa, and Latin America. They culminated in the World Conference on Cultural Policies, or MONDIACULT, in Mexico City in 1982, attended by 960 participants from 126 States. MONDIACULT's major policy "deliverables" were the Mexico City Declaration on Cultural Policies and the recommendation that the United Nations declare a World Decade for Cultural Development, which it did, from 1988 to 1997. These conversations and publications backed a burgeoning institutional administrative establishment. UNESCO urged member nations to grow their cultural bureaucracies and to develop robust, carefully planned cultural policies based on sustained study and comparative observation, aided by UNESCO's own statistics-gathering capacities.

Why did the official vocabulary and institutions of cultural policy arise when they did, to become such a focus for UNESCO as an institution of global governance? What the records of the meetings overwhelmingly suggest is that they were a site of identification for people interested in softening and humanizing an otherwise indifferently imperializing capitalism. Most of those integrally involved in the cultural policy moment were worried that national governments were insufficiently interested in "preserving" culture, whether against the threat of mass media and mass cultural experiences or against the aggressive drive of modernization. They were increasingly interested, especially, in the threats posed to precapitalist postcolonial enclaves that were being integrated into their respective national capitalist economies and into the global economic system.

According to Carole Rosenstein, UNESCO's cultural policy has tended to highlight the ways in which culture is threatened, unevenly developed, and unevenly distributed.[2] This is no doubt true. It is also the case that, from the late 1960s on, and especially so by the later 1970s, a strong cultural policy establishment was treated as a way to counter, discipline, and humanize capitalism. Culture itself was simply defined as a means of "humanizing" economic development. The 1967 Paris roundtable stipulates somewhat blandly that "culture should be linked to the fulfilment of personality and to economic and social development."[3] Economic development is presented largely as a positive movement toward personal fulfillment. But as the cultural policy discussions went on throughout the 1970s, the temptation became stronger and stronger to imagine that the course of capitalist development needed to be corrected with recourse to "culture."

We can account for this shift in emphasis in a few ways. As René Maheu's term as director general (1962–1974) gave way to that of Amadou-Mahtar M'Bow (1974–1987), and as the many economic crises of the era took hold—energy, currency, oil, banking, Third World debt—what began as a lament over the inaccessibility of high art turned into a lament over the growing poverty rates. What began as an insistence that economic development is itself crucial to "elevating" the cultural level became a deep suspicion about the very language of growth and achievement. Worry about possible debasement via mass culture became more and more muted; the insistence that all people need the foundational conditions of existence that would allow them meaningful cultural expression—and not just meaningful cultural expression, but meaningful life—was amplified instead.

Maheu was French, maintained generally good relations with the United States, and was committed to the project of democratizing the conditions conducive to the appreciation of elite cultural goods. Consider one of the most popular programs that flourished under his leadership, the Archives of Colour Reproductions of Paintings, with its attendant *Catalogue of Colour Reproductions* and Travelling Exhibitions of Colour Reproductions. Enabled by technological developments in color reproduction and silk-screen printing, this program used its democratizing capacities largely to teach distant audiences about the wonders of European art, especially French. Unsurprisingly, its aims overlapped considerably with those of the French Ministry of Culture, founded by Charles de Gaulle in the late 1950s and headed by André Malraux until 1969. The culture ministry's declared mission was "to make accessible to the greatest possible number of Frenchmen the great works of humanity, *and particularly those of France.*"[4] A novelist, art historian, and cultural bureaucrat, Malraux had spoken at the opening session of UNESCO's first General Conference, held at the Sorbonne in Paris in 1946, delivering a lecture in which he introduced his idea, soon to be famous, of the "museum without walls": "our Imaginary Museum, worldwide in its scope, will confront us, for the first time, with the plastic inheritance of all mankind."[5] The idea of the "museum without walls" inspired and sustained the Archives of Colour Reproductions project, which was in practice less the neutral clearinghouse implied in the phrase "of all mankind" and more what Rachel Perry described as a European-led program for "exporting [culture] centrifugally out from what Malraux would have called the cradle of civilization to its peripheral outposts."[6]

Or consider the work of Fereydoun Hoveyda, an Iranian intellectual and career diplomat who in the 1960s wrote novels that in part work to justify his commitment to the United Nations and to UNESCO. Hoveyda had impeccable cosmopolitan credentials. He was born in Damascus to an Iranian diplomat, educated in the best French schools in Beirut, flirted with leftist and anticolonial political movements during his formative years, and studied for his PhD in international law and economics at the Sorbonne. Hoveyda was given the opportunity to work alongside his professor, the renowned jurist René Cassin, just as Cassin was involved in preparations for the San Francisco conference at which the United Nations was officially established and as he was working on drafting what was to become the Universal Declaration of Human Rights. After completing his doctorate, Hoveyda remained in Paris as a press attaché at the

Iranian embassy before joining UNESCO in 1951, where he worked until 1966 in the Department of Mass Communications. There he was tasked with facilitating the development of technologies and legal frameworks to secure a better flow of information in the developing countries. During his time at UNESCO, Hoveyda started to write for *Les cahiers du cinéma*; later, he also worked in the film industry, writing screenplays for filmmakers including Roberto Rossellini, with whom he collaborated on *India: Matri Bhumi* (1959), a strange hybrid combining a documentary anthropological tour of India with brief fictional vignettes intended to illuminate the country's defining mythos.

During this time, Hoveyda also wrote his debut novel, *Les Quarantaines* (1962), which became the first book by a non-French person to be nominated for the Prix Goncourt. The novel's setting is a dinner party held at a Parisian mansion during the Algerian Revolution. Its emphasis is on the experiences of an Egyptian guest, Samy Salem, who had been educated in France and now feels caught between the culture of his birth and the values of his new Western milieu. His reflection on the party, which is attended by wealthy, artistic Europeans, leads him to embrace his position as the only person equipped to mediate between conflicting and at times contradictory forces: France versus Algeria; West versus East; peaceful embrace of the heights of civilization versus revolutionary fervor. The novel is committed to what it takes to embody progressive French modernity, while also holding on to the Arab world's traditions. It advocates an international cosmopolitan purview as the only one from which an intellectual elite might truly mediate conflict and pave the road from the age of empire to that of peaceful sovereign nationhood.

In a subsequent novel, *Dans une terre étrange* (1967), a young boy prone to fantasy is changed forever when he sees an 8mm projector in a store window and understands that his love of film and vibrant imagination can become his vocation. He connects possession of the camera with adulthood, as a means of turning his fantastical imaginings into creative productions. The novel thus links access to technology with development toward mature humanity, free creative self-expression, and modernity. It upholds the boy's commitment to a development narrative in which access to and engagement with technology is key to artistry, creativity, and personal and political maturity. Taken together, *Les Quarantaines* and *Dans une terre étrange* can be said to advocate technological modernity and respect for tradition, a cosmopolitan internationalism organized by secular French modernity and committed to distinct national sovereignties, and the crucial affordances of creative self-expression and innovation: in other words, a perfect encapsulation of UNESCO's general world view at the time of Maheu's leadership.

The report that resulted from the 1967 cultural policy roundtable states that "in certain developing societies it is considered that cultural development is essential in order to strengthen awareness of nationhood and thus facilitate the growth of an original culture which will meet both the deepest aspirations of the people and the requirements of the modern world."[7] It elaborates further that in the developing countries, "it is necessary to supervise or simply to guide and advise amateurs in order to avoid the danger of mediocrity, since examples worthy of being followed are not yet distributed widely enough there."[8] We notice a worry, then, about helping people meet their aspirations for cultural expression.

In the late 1960s, the tendency to worry about the threat of mass culture and the debasement of elite modes was still primary at UNESCO. Commercialization and Americanization were key pejoratives. The prevailing sense was that cultures being progressively integrated into global networks of communication and trade needed special attention and protection, funded by their governments, or else they would risk having their cultural particularity annihilated by the onslaught of a foreign mass media with which they could not hope to compete. Only this special attention would ensure their successful transition into modernity and provide the foundation for substantial cultural elevation. Witness, again, Yasunari Kawabata's Nobel Prize, perfect evidence of how attractive laments over commercialism and the destruction of authentic cultures were to literary intellectuals in the late 1960s.

M'Bow, for his part, worked very differently. He wanted UNESCO to give priority to the everyday struggles of the world's poor in the developing nations. He focused less on how to use technological advances to develop the capacity for aesthetic appreciation and more on the alleviation of basic poverty—material, communicative, and cultural. It was under his direction that UNESCO entered into its most radical phase as an organization—so radical that the United States felt compelled to withdraw from it in 1984. In a context of destabilizing economic convulsions and the growing concern that the World Bank and other development institutions existed only to benefit the already developed economies, there formed a new voting block in the United Nations and UNESCO, calling for a New International Economic Order and a New World Information and Communications Order. The next chapter will return to these formations. Suffice it to note here that their target was the iniquitous distribution of wealth and self-serving investment and development schemes. "Cultural development" became in this context a polyvalent catchphrase indicting the development establishment and the dominant role of the United States and its supporters within UNESCO.

At UNESCO, appeals to cultural development usually reflected a drive toward more authentic and sustainable economic integration, in order to bring the postcolonial nations into a reformed global economy that would distribute wealth in a more "balanced" manner. Part of negotiating this integration was holding up aesthetic traditions of precapitalist life as sites of holistic values—as a fundamentally distinguishing and humanizing uniqueness, which is valuable both for its own sake and also as a model for how to organize social life. The report of the Intergovernmental Conference on Cultural Policies in Africa, held in Accra in 1975, engages at length with the particularity of the cultural situation for African nations, which are described as containing important pockets of precapitalist integrity:

> At the cultural level, the very fact that these original societies have remained virtually beyond the fringe of colonization has meant that mother tongues are the only languages used. . . . The family is the essential bearer of these original cultures and the custodian of tradition, in whose transmission it plays a vital part. . . . From time immemorial tradition has affected every aspect of human activity. . . . The safeguarding of values, the restoration of languages, identity—these are the causes in whose behalf resistance has been organized and the struggle for liberation waged. African cultures have pointed the way to individual self-rediscovery and national restoration, reconstruction and mobilization. Of particular significance is the fact that the quest for freedom has coincided, throughout the whole of Africa, with the quest for cultural identity: to assert one's personality is to perform an act of liberation.[9]

Here authentic human freedom is said to entail the development and flourishing of unique cultural identities, and these identities themselves emerge from traditions which, because they may not be compatible with modernization, require safeguarding. By codifying such views, UNESCO helped to mobilize culture as a means of managing the fact that the resonance or purchase of "immemorial" traditions was being threatened by the creeping spread of capitalist commodity markets. These traditions, then, clearly needed to be preserved by institutions like UNESCO, and whatever became outmoded or museumized would need also to be replaced and supplemented with other kinds of meaning making, other kinds of meaningful culture that would sustain the people who were living through these dramatic transformations.

UNESCO was just one of a spectrum of international organizations becoming interested in the idea of cultural development starting in the late 1960s. It was an idea with many facets—some incompatible with one another. Cultural development could mean a culturally attuned and sensitive approach to economic development. It could mean an approach to economic development that was focused on its cultural accompaniments—the attitudes designed to ease the path to economic growth, whether by fostering growth-oriented values or by treating the traumas that can arise when change is rapid. It could also mean development of cultural production specifically, of cultural resources and cultural industries. Private US foundations and state-based American diplomacy even imagined that programs to preserve cultural monuments might quiet political unease. A brief look at their efforts will clarify the relative radicalism of UNESCO's comparable activities.

Kathleen McCarthy describes cultural development as the core paradigm that displaced the very different approach to culture that had characterized the Cold War years in the United States. Within American foundations and State Department programs in the 1960s, the failure to successfully economically integrate both racialized inner cities and peripheral former colonies had occasioned a generally "chastened mood."[10] Cultural development appeared to be a possible solution—a way of making sure that development was "tailored" to local capacities and conditions and of controlling some of the fallout from modernization.[11] McCarthy quotes Ford Foundation officials who hoped that they could help developing nations to "cope constructively with rapid change in ways that leave individuals whole and societies relatively peaceful," and who were motivated by the idea that they might help to counter anomie by providing what McCarthy describes as "enduring touchstones," such as protected monuments to cultural heritage, as a means of improving, if not people's material circumstances, then at least their "quality of life." They thought that by training local scholars and conservators to protect cultural monuments and legacies as evidence of authentic indigenous cultural activity, they might help to prop up national pride. This approach unseated the older and more aggressive path to economic development, which ostensibly saw the values of the past only as impediments to achieving the prize of modernity. Cultural development meant using the past respectfully, to frame the present in ways that could help people deal with the trauma of the movement from tradition to modernity. The past was not "a mere obstacle to modernization" but rather, in the words of a Ford Foundation officer, "a source of dignity and worth, to be explored and constructed in the present and carried forward proudly in the national future." In the late 1960s and early 1970s, specific Ford Foundation programs for cultural development therefore aimed to prevent the destruction of cultural artefacts and sites, saving them so that they could instead ground cultural pride, become resources for education and for museums, and support the development of tourism infrastructure.[12]

Even the World Bank, which in its first years had been strictly focused on brick-and-mortar projects, was increasingly interested in cultural development and willing to fund educational infrastructure. In 1964, Gary Becker published *Human Capital*, which aimed to assess the "tremendous amount of circumstantial evidence testifying to the economic importance of human capital, especially education." Becker's conclusion, that "human capital is going to be an important part of the thinking about development, income distribution, labor turnover, and many other problems for a long time to come," proved inordinately prescient.[13] UNESCO was itself one of the agencies that had already been amassing "circumstantial evidence" about the causal link between economic development and investment in education. But the idea was of course crucial to the entire development establishment, which consistently assumed that modernized industry would naturally go hand in hand with more advanced levels of education. Theodore Schultz, who had used the term "human capital theory" in a 1960 presidential address to the American Economic Association, helped to persuade George Woods, then president of the World Bank, that "educational investments were a necessary complement to investments in industry, infrastructure and agriculture."[14] Influenced by the growing acceptance of human capital theory, Woods conceded that investment in education might result in some returns.

Robert McNamara, who was appointed president of the World Bank in 1968, in turn oversaw an era of relatively healthy investment in "occupational education," which was a form of targeted training meant to increase worker productivity. Occupational education was very much akin to the functional literacy training that the US commission to UNESCO preferred, as a rule, to fundamental literacy programs. Fundamental literacy—sometimes called "traditional" literacy—presents literacy as a human right and a goal of its own, as part of an individual's inherent personal development, irrespective of job skills. The more targeted, functional literacy that the United States preferred to support was a form of technical assistance linked directly to economic development. It was aimed at developing a particular set of skills rather than encouraging a general expansion. Walter Rostow, the US National Security Advisor—who was also the author of one of the development industry's bibles, *The Four Stages of Growth*—warned against making any special contribution to UNESCO's fundamental literacy work. Rostow was opposed to mass literacy campaigns; he would only support "limited efforts to link literacy with technical and vocational training and specific mechanisms for free market economic growth" and worried that "raising the educational levels of the poor was dangerous in emerging economies that could not guarantee full employment."[15]

McNamara was, for his part, a prolific proponent of the idea that poverty leads to communism. He argued that "the only way to fight socialism around the world was to raise the living standards of the poor and soften the worst inequalities created and perpetuated by capitalism."[16] "Given the certain connection between economic stagnation and the incidence of violence," McNamara wrote, "the years that lie ahead for the nations of the southern half of the globe look ominous. . . . Communist nations are capable of subverting, manipulating and finally directing for their own ends the wholly legitimate grievances of a developing society."[17] Backed by such thinking, his presidency of the World Bank, lasting thirteen years, ushered in an unprecedented era of lending for projects based on a new model called "redistribution with growth." Redistribution with growth aimed to meet what the United Nations, at the same time, labeled "basic needs." Redistribution with growth was focused on improving living standards for the poor in developing nations, and it included "massive funding of primary education, with World Bank lending increasing from $883 million per year in 1968 to $12 billion per year in 1981."[18] But because loans for primary education would have to be repaid, it was hoped that governments would use the funds efficiently and prioritize building the economy. Educational lending for basic literacy was justified as an investment in future human capital rather than as, say, a fundamental human right, or a conduit to anyone's political awakening.

As director general of UNESCO, Maheu had been on board with the United States' preferred approach to literacy development and oversaw UNESCO's turn toward functional literacy campaigns. In 1967, he wrote: "Now that it is realized that illiteracy is a factor in underdevelopment, literacy teaching is conversely gaining recognition as a factor in development."[19] Indeed, UNESCO's Experimental World Literacy Program (EWLP), which lasted from 1966 to 1974, arose as a sort of concession to American opposition to a Soviet-backed Ukrainian proposal to the United Nations General Assembly for "a massive, global attack on adult illiteracy." The American commission to UNESCO could only tolerate the conception of literacy that the World Bank also preferred: as an investment in human capital that would eventually back further economic growth. The EWLP was functionalist and was developed under pressure from the United States. The programs that were established, with support from the United Nations Development Program, in Algeria, Ecuador, Ethiopia, Guinea, Iran, Madagascar, Mali, Sudan, Tanzania, India, and Syria were predominantly vocational: "Almost 90 percent of EWLP learners, for instance, were educated for the direct purposes of agricultural and industrial development."[20]

In the mid-1970s, the EWLP was evaluated in a UNESCO interim report, which describes the principles underlying functional literacy at some length, in part to establish that there is a difference in kind between functional and fundamental, or "traditional," literacy training. It is a fascinating document, not least because, while stating that the EWLP has been somewhat successful in achieving its goals, it tends to imply that there is some reason to worry about the goals themselves. Functional literacy, the report states:

> claims to be a method of improving the productive capacities of man as a worker by enabling him to acquire, through the medium of reading and writing, the theoretical and practical knowledge needed for a development "project." In a process of this kind, reading and writing constitute not an end in itself but a means—and a fundamentally important one—to the intellectualization, mental grasp and interiorization of technical knowledge, the mastering of the thought-language relationship which can facilitate the transition from thinking in concrete terms, when explanations tend to be sought in magic, to thinking in abstract terms, when the mind is receptive to the scientific interpretation of phenomena.[21]

This description suggests very clearly that functional literacy is more than just exposure to a capacity. It is rather induction into an ideology, specifically designed to accompany a planned development scheme. Functional literacy training is, in the further words of the interim report, "a complex process of technical advancement, scientific acculturation and social and cultural integration, constituting a global educational operation which contributes to changing and gaining mastery of the milieu."[22] In its detailing of the specific ends of such training schemes, the report reinforces claims made in the records of the cultural policy meetings discussed above. It suggests that functional literacy has been developed not in the service of general human flourishing and autonomous development, but rather to facilitate the incorporation of societies "undergoing change" into an uneven global economic whole.

A final EWLP evaluation, published two years later, is considerably less sanguine about the results of the approach, while still not totally prepared to say that the whole program had been politically noxious or a failure. Though Dorn and Ghodsee suggest that the assessment exists to impugn the EWLP as, basically, an imperializing imposition, in fact the report's conclusions are better described as ambivalent. The report states that the functionalist approach:

> reflects the view prevalent in United Nations and Western academic circles at the beginning of the First Development Decade [lasting from 1960 to 1970], that development was first and foremost a question of economic growth, stressing capital-intensive development and high-level technical skills. From this point of view, education in general and literacy in particular were considered as means of "developing" the "underdeveloped" people in terms of giving them the knowledge and skills necessary to expend their "potential capital in the services of society."[23]

Two basic truths are ignored by this view, the report continues: "First, a human being cannot be 'underdeveloped.' Secondly, the relative underdevelopment of certain economies is a partial result of the iniquities of the prevailing world economic system."[24] Having acknowledged, though, that underdevelopment is a way of thinking about human beings that has no fundamental validity, and that what causes economic underdevelopment is the organization of the world system rather than the absence within a given population of certain kinds of literacy, and having noted that for these very reasons functional literary instruction was being challenged in the late 1960s and early 1970s, the authors are nevertheless careful to stress that they do not mean to "discredit economically functional literacy in general." They mean rather to "question narrowly productivity-centred functionality" because what they describe as a broader "economic literacy," which would entail "stressing critical awareness of the producer-learner's problems and roles in society," would better support UNESCO's own commitments to a humanistic rather than economistic world view.[25] Clearly, this EWLP assessment is not a statement of opposition to capitalist development, but rather expresses an interest in building the best capacities to respond to and autonomously direct that development. What had to be acknowledged and factored into literacy training was thus the importance of not just "economic growth" but the "social, cultural and political change" that attend it.

Both the growing investment in the cultural development paradigm and the parallel rise of and reckoning with functional literacy training suggest the way in which voices speaking out against top-down developmentalism were emboldened throughout the 1970s by the crises plaguing the advanced democracies. Crisis-ridden states were interested in funding things that had once been considered beyond the pale, like primary education and the training of professional heritage curators and conservationists. Their development agencies were desperate to ensure more effective economic integration or at least to foster the impression that they cared about the maldistribution of wealth. Meanwhile, for every advanced capitalist welfare state talking about meeting people's basic needs, there was a representative to UNESCO from one of the developing economies insisting that they would not let "culture" be traduced for the sake of adding more wealth to economies that seemed woefully inattentive to actual human needs.

We see, then, how one could use the language of cultural development and investment in human capital to encourage funding for the preservation of monuments and technical training in the policy and museum sectors as a means, ultimately, of reconciling people to the psychic strains of modernization. Or one could use it to impugn the dominance of economic reason in determining the course of world affairs. On the one hand, at the World Bank and at other US-based organs of development logic, when the role of culture and education did become, to a limited extent, recognized and supported, it was for clearly expedient reasons. It could be seen as a means of readying people for work: the poor are more likely to turn to communism, and productive labor is ennobling and important to a flourishing economy. Or it could be seen as a matter of teaching people how to appreciate their own cultural heritage, their own history, in a way that is not too aggressive or protectionist, or too averse to modernizing forces. On the other hand, within UNESCO, the critique of developmentalism became the dominant perspective for a time, competing with the American approach. A humanizing cultural legacy was put forward as a foundational right that all people could claim, regardless of their current employment status or future prospects. Culture was positioned as a source of non-commodified values that are especially important for states to protect and foster; indeed, having a "cultural" purview came to mean something like "acknowledging that people shouldn't be left to starve just because they aren't in paid employment." It was possible at UNESCO to imagine culture as a humanizing answer to the depredations of developmentalist capitalism, as the parties to the cultural policy meetings seized the opportunity, presented especially by the waning hegemony of the United States, to establish their own claims to legitimate governance. They established these claims by an affiliation with culture, which was in turn defined as constitutively humanizing.

In his opening address to the 1982 MONDIACULT conference, Fernando Solana (who chaired the committee charged with drafting the Mexico City Declaration on Cultural Policies, the major policy guideline resulting from the conference) emphasized general conditions:

> Between 1970 and the present day we have witnessed increasing progress in science and technology, in education and communication. And we have seen improvement in the living conditions of thousands of the world's communities. Nevertheless, we have also witnessed the crisis of the international economic systems created during the Second World War; we have seen the economic problems, those of unemployment, inflation and lack of food production.[26]

He lamented that "the triumph of production" had "not signified a triumph for mankind." In the affluent countries, there were millions of people jobless. In the poorer nations there were "still more than 800 million illiterate adults," while "half of the world's inhabitants consume[d] daily less food than [was] required for an acceptable diet." He stated that as a result of unequal development, "it is as though we were living in all the centuries of history at once. There are human beings who are born, eat, live and die just as they would have done two hundred or two thousand years ago. Others are living in the world of the future; they produce, consume, create under conditions determined by the highest levels of progress." He described this, and the underlying tension between what he called technical and ethical progress, as "the fundamental contradiction" of the age.[27]

Solana claimed that in the prevailing dispensation, all that was developed was "systems to produce more things and institutions to operate systems to produce more things." What was really needed instead was the development of "knowledge and values," which would counsel people to produce only those things that were really needed and would cultivate "their creativity, their control over their own destinies." Desire for economic growth is ongoing and totally legitimate, he argued, but how far? "How can economic growth be reformed," he asked, "so that it is rational, proportionate to the availability of natural resources geared to the satisfaction of real needs, regulated by decisions that take into account the well-being of all . . . ?" This is the role of culture. Indeed, Solano defined culture quite precisely—and in words that were then echoed in the Mexico Declaration on Cultural Policy that he helped write—as "man's capacity for reflection on himself."[28] Cultural policy must therefore set itself the task of "rectifying" the deviation from the human in the development process. In his closing address to the conference, M'Bow added his voice to Solana's, stating that the goal of all cultural policy supported by UNESCO should be "to humanize development by restoring to it its cultural aims."[29]

It is an unusual assertion, I know, but attention to the legitimacy crises of the hegemonic states is crucial to understanding UNESCO's cultural policy at the time. If a healthy labor market is one condition of loyalty to the welfare state, as well as being the vital source of its taxation-based revenues, then it is no wonder that when these conditions are no longer so secure, the manufacture of loyalty becomes a worry. The process of collective regulation—including the production of legitimacy—that is required to ensure the survival of capitalist exchange becomes more apparent. Collective regulation is expensive, too, thus increasing even further the contradiction between the permanent fiscal deficits now plaguing the advanced welfare state governments and the need to spend in order to manage social problems. As scholars observed at the time, governmental efforts to manage crises become subject to their own crisis tendencies. What arises is a dynamic of declining growth and increased need for social regulation—a so-called "demand overload" that states with growing permanent fiscal deficits are less and less able to meet.[30]

UNESCO built the legitimacy of its own policy-making function on the grounds of these crises. It offered, to those states that felt themselves aggrieved by the dominant economic order, an opportunity to exploit the aura of illegitimacy around those hegemonic forces and to stake their own claim to legitimacy—a legitimacy extending both to their own state governments and to UNESCO as a branch of world government. They staked those claims by an affiliation with humanism, culture, and cultural development. In other words, when official national governments so clearly appeared to be illegitimate bearers of "humane" capacities, agencies of cultural policy, including UNESCO, stepped in as sites for the expression of the will toward de-commodification—meaning, simply, the state-backed rescue of certain human practices and supports from being reduced to commodity status. The cultural policy moment is precisely an expression and codification of this will. For this reason, cultural policy can only be partially grasped through the idea that it is a minor pocket of governance engaged in helping to discipline subjects. It is also one of the premiere de-commodifying wings available to governance, where concerns about the needs left unmet by capitalism are articulated and worked out. At UNESCO, the moment of the turn toward cultural policy is a sign of the organization, as a global intergovernmental agency, having become an outlet for concerns about the truths of global economic integration and the insufficiency and hypocrisy of national social policies, including international development policies, when those fail to live up to their promises and their fissures become impossible to ignore.

* * *

In the same way that the English translation of *Snow Country* crystallizes the politics of the postwar policy milieu at UNESCO, Tayeb Salih's short story "The Doum Tree of Wad Hamid" offers a suggestive engagement with, and support for, the cultural policy work that occurred there from the late 1960s on. It was published in Arabic in 1966 and in English in 1968. Like Salih's more celebrated novel, *Seasons of Migration to the North*, the story plays on tensions between rural and urban, West and East, tradition and modernity, integral to Salih's own intellectual development and working life. Salih was born in a small rural village in what became Sudan, but left a life of subsistence farming to become one of a small number of people educated at a middle school in Port Sudan, where he learned English. He went from there to a British-built secondary school—one of only two secondary schools in the country at the time.

Salih then moved to England to take a job working for the BBC's Arabic Service, where he eventually headed the drama division. He was later a director of the Ministry of Information in Qatar, before settling into UNESCO in Paris, where he worked in various capacities, including as a representative of the Arab states, until his retirement. My suggestion here is not that "The Doum Tree of Wad Hamid" reflects Salih's time at UNESCO; in fact, he did not go to work there until later in his life. It is rather that the story registers the concerns of a person who was involved and invested in the possibilities of cultural administration and policy making, and whose work—literary and otherwise—was about the pressures that attend the incorporation of the precapitalist enclaves that were integral to the global cultural policy moment. The story is an example of the pervasiveness of a certain way of thinking; it explores, explains, and tries to justify the kind of subjective life that could find something like UNESCO's production of world heritage sites useful. It is part of the activity that validates the cultural policy establishment.

"The Doum Tree of Wad Hamid" is in fact about a moment of cultural policy. The story is a narrative within a narrative, featuring a younger man who is not from Wad Hamid telling about listening to a village elder describe the relationship that the villagers have to the doum tree. They practice an unorthodox kind of Islam in the village, focused on the doum tree and its mythic origins and healing properties. The tomb of Wad Hamid is itself said to be buried beneath the tree, at its very roots. The village is relatively poor and its inhabitants uninterested in any relationship with either the newly formed Sudanese national government or any more official religious organizations.

The story is about both what the old man says and how the younger man processes what he learns. We rarely hear from the young man as narrator until the memorable end of the story, in which he describes the significant emotional effect that the old man's story has had on him. The distinction between orality and literacy—our constant consciousness that we are meant to imagine that we are reading a transcription of the man's oral tale—is not incidental to the story as a whole; it is one of many expressions of the fundamental tension between tradition and modernity that Salih intended to note. In Salih's work for the BBC Arabic Service, he was often himself in a position not unlike that of the young man, traveling as a correspondent and talking to people from all walks of life.

The old man recounts when the village became of interest to the government of the new postcolonial nation, and we see how this represents the village's first insertion into the order of modernity and developmentalism, though the old man doesn't use such vocabulary, surely unfamiliar to him. Officials had come to visit the village, hoping to set up first a water pump and agricultural scheme and then a steamer stop, so that the village could be made a part of the logistical and practical order of a new, urbanizing world. But the proposed location of the water pump and then the steamer stop was of course precisely where the doum tree is located, high on a natural promontory. As the privileged object of the villagers' faith, the doum tree is sacrosanct. The old man recounts stories of the villagers' dreams about the tree healing them in times of illness; he talks about how the tree gives shade to the entire village and how everyone in the village lives and dies aware of the tree's constant presence. The young visitor asks how the tree came to be there, and the old man demurs: the tree cannot be conscripted into a narrative of development. Like the village itself, from which it cannot be meaningfully distinguished, it is the opposite of the order of development. No one remembers a time when it didn't exist, and no one can imagine a world without it. "Other places begin by being small and then grow larger," he tells the visitor, "but this village of ours came into being at one bound. Its population neither increases nor decreases, while its appearance remains unchanged. And ever since our village has existed, so has the doum tree of Wad Hamid."[31]

The proposals to cut down the tree for the sake of a water pump or a steamer stop are for this reason startling and unconscionable to the villagers, and they collectively eject the agents of the new state government. Their ejection is on one occasion so forceful, however, that they are taken off to jail, and so become embroiled in a political conflict between the first postcolonial government and a new, second, administration which is currently in power. The original government uses the cause of the villagers of Wad Hamid to assert its love for the Sudanese people—a category of belonging that is of no interest to the jailed villagers—in a political fight against the party that usurped the power of the first government. Seeking to return to power in order to direct the course of the new postcolonial state, the old government thus instrumentalizes the ideal of the villagers' resistance to state coercion and declares itself on the side of the common folk. The people in the city where the jail is located soon take up the cause and protest outside the jail for the villagers' release. All the villagers know is that when, after a short time, they are freed, there are some posh-looking people in clean clothes and gold watches cheering them as they walk out. They only learn of the nature of the whole political imbroglio from a later visitor who is "cast upon" them in the village, who recounts a newspaper report of the former leader's "fiery speech" in Parliament: "To such tyranny has this government come that it has begun to interfere in the beliefs of the people, in those holy things held most sacred by them. . . . Ask our worthy Prime Minister about the doum tree of Wad Hamid. Ask him how it was that he permitted himself to send his troops and henchmen to desecrate that pure and holy place!" (17–18). As a result of this mobilization of the Wad Hamid villagers' cause, the ostensible tyrants fall and the first government returns to power, with the major national newspaper declaring the doum tree of Wad Hamid "the symbol of the nation's awakening" (18).

As a way to recognize the role the village played in its return to power, the new government, which had been the old government not long before, puts a fence around the doum tree and an interpretive plaque explaining why it is such an important symbol of the dignity and uniqueness of the Sudanese people. The old man describes the plaque, along with the stone pedestal it stands on, as "the only new things about the village since God first planted it here" (14)—a symbol and sign of developmentalist teleology. Here we have our moment of origin for cultural policy. A government seeking to solidify its claim to legitimate rule idealizes the uniqueness of a regional tradition and places a sacred object in a new order of meaning. It celebrates a symbol of anti-aspirational anti-development but, in the process, serves to accomplish (if only in a small way) something that the old man and his fellow villagers had been completely uninterested in: the incorporation of the rural village into the national narrative.

In *Caliban and the Witch*, Silvia Federici describes living in Nigeria during the period of its first Structural Adjustment Program (SAP) imposed by the International Monetary Fund and the World Bank, lasting from 1984 to 1986. The goal of the SAP was ostensibly to make Nigeria a competitive player in global markets, and achieving this goal clearly involved what "The Doum Tree of Wad Hamid" describes as being imposed by force in a different local context. In Federici's terms, this was "a new round of primitive accumulation, and a rationalization of social reproduction aimed at destroying the last vestiges of communal property and community relations, and thereby impos[ing] more intense forms of labor exploitation."[32] The style of argument in *Caliban and the Witch* is partly inspired by the parallels that struck Federici, linking her research subject to her current context in Nigeria. She had set out to study the burning of witches as a manifestation of the way in which proletarianization transformed gender relations, as the proletarian male was in part reconciled to his loss of access to the commons by his control over women as a new common property whose sexuality was then policed and punished when wayward. The primitive accumulation and destruction of communal property that Federici witnessed appeared to her as a clear revelation of a fundamental ungovernability: "how limited is the victory that the capitalist work-discipline has won on this planet," she writes, "and how many people still see their lives in ways radically antagonistic to the requirements of capitalist production."[33]

The same emphases emerge in Salih's story. This persistent and ineradicable antagonism is part of what UNESCO's cultural programming has consistently

helped to acknowledge, integrate, manage, and assuage. The source of the transformations that UNESCO has sought to manage through its cultural programming is not only the more immediate context of economic crisis and crises of
governmental legitimacy but also the permanent and ongoing deeper crisis of
the integration into capitalist modernity of precapitalist enclaves that are always
potentially ungovernable.

In Salih's story, the villagers become subjects of governance in spite of their
resistance, but only to a degree. Their indifference to the idea of the state and their
adherence to village community priorities and ideals remains in force. They are
ungovernable, still; the fence and plaque are not, after all, for them—they hardly
need the tree to be interpreted to them—but for nationalist ideologues and sundry
tourists. The presence of the plaque and fence would seem to place a distance between them and their sacred icon, but the old man doesn't register a fundamental
shift in those terms. He tells the young man that they simply now have a fence
and a plaque that neither transform nor impinge upon the tree. These come from
a world of modernization, where objects are removed from their specific contexts
and placed into new national narratives—museumized, as it were. The old man
rejects any worry that the villagers' relationship to the tree might be ruined by the
process. The new items aren't relevant to the old.

The worry that does exist, though, is precisely the young man's worry, and of
course it is meant to be ours. The young man begins to conclude his report on
the old man's story with an account of his asking the old man when the village
will change its ways. The old man says that the village will change when generations of young people, like the man reporting his story to us, leave their villages,
have their souls disciplined by modernity, and thus stop wanting to suffer the
apparent ills of poor village life, so that, finally, the doum tree no longer appears
in their dreams. The young man is inspired by this to inquire further: when will
the village agree to enter into the process of development by accepting the new
water pump, agricultural scheme, and steamer stop, since they have, after all, accepted the plaque and the fence? The old man's answer comes as a surprise here.
He says, "there's plenty of room for all these things: the doum tree, the tomb, the
water-pump, and the steamer's stopping-place" (19).

It is here that the story becomes most clearly an expression of what seems
to have been a fundamentally agreed-upon world view at UNESCO at the time,
registering the very dilemmas that the moment of codification of cultural policy
sought to manage. After saying that there is room for everything in the village,

the old man gives the young man an indescribable look, which, the young man says, "stirred within me a feeling of sadness, sadness for some obscure thing which I was unable to define" (19–20). What do this ineffable look, and the resulting sadness, signify? The old man's words suggest that the steamer stop could have been set up all along, no big deal, if the official agents of development had simply asked the villagers where it might be best placed. Instead, they showed up with their plan already set and, as outsiders, sought to impose it upon the people who lived there day to day. It was a problem of external imposition; a negotiation with local representatives could have averted the whole conflict to begin with.

In this way, the story seems, in its final moments, to be about making development a local affair, with experts from outside listening to and respecting the will of the local community. It positions micro-narratives of local needs against the classic macro-narrative of national development and progress. It recommends that communities develop autonomously within the national framework and—by extension—that nations develop autonomously as sovereign states within the global whole. The story captures perfectly UNESCO's own desire to negotiate localism and globalism, tradition and modernity, blueprint development and its fragmentation into humane, sensitized, culturalized forms—that is, into "cultural development." But it is also a fantasy, perhaps a compensatory one.

The story imagines a fantastical reconciliation of villages like Wad Hamid with the inevitability of development, in which the villages might be modernized without threatening the community's traditional ways of life. The old man's vision of this reconciliation sits oddly with his own admission that more and more young people are leaving the village, that there is some inevitability to the demise of the tree's ongoing presence in the dream lives of future generation. Perhaps that's the meaning of his indescribable look: he is registering the misfit between his faith in the possible coexistence of tradition and modernity and his acknowledgment that the village cannot survive the development process, with young people leaving farming behind to join the workforce and buy gold watches. Nor does his story of the government's instrumentalization of the villagers' traditional ungovernability inspire much hope.

As listeners to the villager's story, finally, we are asked to register his experiences somewhere within our modernized world views and—the old man asks—not to judge him "too harshly." We are even offered a possible disposition toward the old man's seeming awareness of the inadequacy of his romance of reconciliation with the modernizing postcolonial state. That disposition is sadness. Not to celebrate but to acknowledge, with sadness, the perils of incorporation into the modern world system. Not to celebrate but to acknowledge, with sadness, that the government's first acts of cultural policy serve to conscript people into identification with the new postcolonial nation, using the ideal of the people's inherent sovereignty, difference, and dignity as justification for bringing the village into precisely the thing it resisted: a teleology of national identity and development. Not to celebrate . . . but neither to fight fundamentally against. Simply to acknowledge, with sadness. An affective solution, where no practical, practicable one can be glimpsed. Culture.

Book Hunger

UNESCO HAS, SINCE ITS FOUNDING, amassed considerable statistics about the global book trades. It publishes an annual *Index Translationum*, listing book translations by language and by subject, and a *Statistical Yearbook*, monitoring national levels of import and export of books and other media. In addition to collecting statistics, UNESCO has been a key player in defining what to count and how to count it. It was UNESCO that supported the formulation of the first official definition of a book accepted by the publishing industry: a nonperiodical printed publication of at least forty-nine pages, excluding covering matter. The invention of the International Standard Book Number, or ISBN, to ease the international sale and tracking of titles, was facilitated and backed by UNESCO. International copyright law has been debated, established, and reformed at key UNESCO-backed conferences. UNESCO has also often advocated the treatment of books as a unique category of commodity, which should not be subject to regular tariffs, taxes, or postage. And UNESCO has been at the forefront of efforts to measure and address worldwide illiteracy.

A 1965 issue of the *UNESCO Courier*, the organization's central newsletter, states that

> books permeate the whole of UNESCO's programme to such an extent that it is difficult to isolate and define them as a separate factor. They are basic to the achievement of almost all of the Organization's objectives—universal primary education no less than the mutual appreciation of cultural values or the advancement of science and technology.[1]

This is certainly true. Yet some UNESCO programs have used books more pointedly than others. Here, the Collection of Representative Works can be usefully compared to a second set of programs that emerged in the 1960s, culminating in the designation of 1972 as International Book Year and the attendant publication of an official UNESCO Charter of the Book. The charter, whose ten articles were made available as a poster to be displayed at International Book Year events, advocated views that seemed to UNESCO essential to the task of aiding the global spread of the printed word. These views included, for example: "A sound publishing industry is essential to national development" (article 4) and "Society has a special obligation to establish the conditions in which authors can exercise their creative role" (article 3).[2]

UNESCO's book development initiatives emerged alongside the cultural policy directives discussed in the last chapter, reflecting a new two-thirds majority within UNESCO made up of the recently decolonized and anti-colonial nations. Aimed at feeding what was dubbed "book hunger," these initiatives soon informed UNESCO's more controversial support for an emerging New World Information and Communications Order, which complemented an even more encompassing New International Economic Order debated at the United Nations. For UNESCO at this time, books were essentially one of several mass media within an unevenly developed global communications environment. Many working within UNESCO, or in concert with it, saw this as an environment suited to a handful of wealthy, powerful, content-producing nations and argued that its imbalances could only be righted through significant cooperative intervention on the part of international organizations and national governments.

The research backed by UNESCO, which informed the organization's policy statements and programs, tended to conceive of the book in highly political and embattled terms. Books were positioned as agents of cultural and economic development. By suggesting that the book industries could only be properly understood in relation to such a contested process as "progress," UNESCO made the book industries themselves the subject of intense scrutiny and debate. The majority of those who participated in this debate used their knowledge about how culture is produced, traded, and consumed as the basis for recommendations about how local and global governments might work to mitigate imbalances in capitalist cultural markets. They invested in research so that it could inform policy making and wanted policy itself to be reformist, forceful, and effective.

In devising its policies and activities, UNESCO became, from the late 1950s to the early 1980s, the premiere sponsor, facilitator, and consolidator of research on the book trades, conducting *avant la lettre* what soon emerged as the self-conscious practice of book history and working with scholars who have since been embraced as important influences on that field, such as Lucien Febvre and

Henri-Jean Martin, coauthors of *L'Apparition du livre* (1957). The largest portion of the research that UNESCO supported was about books in the developing world. Philip Altbach's studies of scholarly publishing in the developing world, some of them backed by UNESCO, explored in great detail what he skewered as the Western bias of the international scholarly community.[3] It is perhaps this same bias that placed research like his own on the outskirts of the field, preventing studies of the book in the developing world from actively shaping the early book history canon. Otherwise, why would a discipline concerned with the social, cultural, and economic forces that impinge upon the production and consumption of books have ignored UNESCO's rich and various activities addressing the barriers to the rise of indigenous book industries in the developing world?

Consider the "communications circuit" at the heart of what book historians take as a founding document, Robert Darnton's 1982 article, "What Is the History of Books?" Darnton's suggested circuit is derived from his research on Enlightenment-era France, but he writes that with "minor adjustments, it should apply to all periods in the history of the printed book" and argues that book history's "disparate segments can be brought together within a single conceptual scheme."[4] Darnton's circuit (fig. 1) became the foundational model within the field, informing much of the subsequent scholarship charting the interaction among those deemed to be the circuit's key players, namely authors, publishers, printers, shippers, booksellers, and readers. While Darnton's model is no doubt in some respects a welcome invitation to begin to think about books as material objects that circulate within particular economies, some features of the model made it highly inimical to research on the book in the developing world, and it is also limited as a starting point for any study of the book that seeks an informed place from which to intervene in debates about the iniquitous distribution of cultural and economic resources. The circuit is presented as a neutral depiction of a feedback loop that "transmits messages, transforming them en route, as they pass from thought to writing to printed characters and back to thought again."[5] The visual representation of Darnton's communications circuit seems to ask us to conceive its very center as the "Economic and Social Conjuncture." Yet we see in the absence of any arrows pointing from that conjuncture outward—with arrows signifying effective relationships—the conjuncture's lack of determinative, consequential force. It is less a center than a background, in fact, a background that can or cannot be factored into one's analysis.

Indeed, the article that elucidates how the circuit should be understood relegates to its margins the question of how the circuit's entire functioning relates "with other systems, economic, social, political, and cultural, in the surrounding environment."[6] These "other systems" are not the object of study, analysis, or intervention, in other words. It is rather the circuit itself, connecting the primary actors within the book industries, that is central. Any other features, "economic, social, political, and cultural," are simply the possible context in which the circuit functions, and no particular "system"—no "Economic and Social Conjuncture"—is presented as crucially impinging upon the free agency of the actors who make up the circuit.

Darnton's article also importantly conceives the book trade as a network that has "evolved" toward an ideal symbiosis, in which productive capacities exist to supply the needs of readers who in turn inform what comes to be produced subsequently. The questions that Darnton asks book historians to try to answer suggest the communications circuit's ineluctable "evolution" toward its free functioning as a commercial book trade that meets readers' needs without the menacing interventions of particular individuals or government officials.[7] "At what point did writers free themselves from the patronage of wealthy noblemen and the state in order to live by their pens?" he asks; and what characterizes "the evolution of the publisher as a distinct feature"?[8] Here Darnton presents the book trade in the wealthy Western countries as a highly developed, perfected model, a model in which individual agents freely participate in a market unconstrained

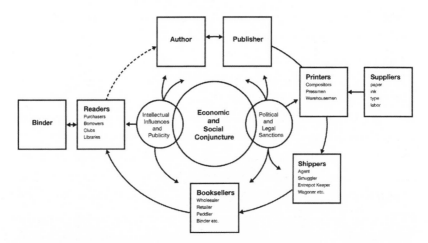

Figure 1. The communications circuit. From Robert Darnton, "What Is the History of Books?" *Daedalus* 111, no. 3 (Summer 1982): 65–83, figure on 68. © 1982 by the American Academy of Arts and Sciences. Reprinted with permission from MIT Press Journals.

by anything other than consumer desire and commercial ingenuity. Despite claiming that book history must necessarily be "international in scope,"[9] the model ignores how the book trade functions outside Europe, while presenting what exists in Europe as the result of centuries of progress toward an ideal order of free-market exchange in which commercial interests work to produce and disseminate enlightened ideas to willing readers.

The studies of the book trades that UNESCO backed have quite a different inflection. They tend to highlight the constitutive roles played by international organizations like UNESCO itself; state-based agencies like the British Council, the Ford Foundation, and the French Ministry of Culture; trade organizations like the International Publishers Association; and aid agencies like the United States Agency for International Development (USAID) and the Soviet State Committee for Foreign Economic Relations, both of which had major competing book donation schemes in place throughout the Cold War period. We have already seen that even the World Bank was involved, as it began by the 1970s to advance perspectives on education, literacy, and development that shaped the kind of aid that the book industries in the developing world would receive. Meanwhile, local book trade representatives appeared before UNESCO because they sought exemptions from international copyright agreements, exemptions that would allow them to publish foreign works in less expensive editions, just as the United States had done when it for many years studiously avoided adhering to the Berne Convention for the Protection of Literary and Artistic Works and thereby built its publishing infrastructure via piracy.[10] If we were to turn all of this thinking about the book and underdevelopment into a Darnton-style model, it would feature not a perfected system of free exchange but rather a complex network of private-sector interests, propped up by state policies supporting the dominance of some and the marginalization of others. Less a circuit, then, than a fortress. Less the free movement of individual agents through a network of voluntary and mutually beneficial exchange, and more a situation where the flourishing of some entails the domination and exclusion of others, with the terms of inclusion being dictated by the hegemonic powers.

Darnton glosses his communications circuit with a definition of book history as "the social and cultural history of communication by print," and writes that "its purpose is to understand how ideas were transmitted through print and how exposure to the printed word affected the thought and behavior of mankind during the last five hundred years."[11] Book history is, for Darnton, concerned with understanding how things have happened in the past, but not with any intent to turn that knowledge into informed policy making. This delimitation of scholarly inquiry to a noninterventionist role, combined with an absence of any reference to how hegemonic power blocs and local and international governments, along with nongovernmental organizations and institutions, shape cultural and economic development, means that Darnton's communications circuit even further affirms the ideal of an unregulated market-based economy. This exact ideal, of an economy made up of autonomous agents unhindered by any influence aside from the market's own logic, is what representatives of the more powerful nations pitted against what the UNESCO Secretariat and the majority of member nations at the time were envisioning. It was one of their sticks. And of course, an emphasis on the ideal of individuals acting without any determination or constraint, voluntarily interacting to advance their own interests in a progressive and propitious circuit, went on to become one of the central affirmations of the neoliberal governance strategies that would begin their global ascent in the early 1980s and become dominant at UNESCO starting in the latter half of that decade.

* * *

In *Human Rights Inc.*, Joseph Slaughter skewers what he calls the "writing man's burden," defined as the "humanitarian injunction" that "reading nations must help nonreading ones (to read)." He writes that after decolonization, a developmentalist attitude, committed to functional and spiritual modernization, "coalesced as the predominant discursive paradigm in the industrialized West." Caught up in this paradigm was the technology of literacy, along with the specific "artifactual form of the book," which became, in Slaughter's words, "something of a fetish within certain humanitarian strands of developmentalist discourse and human rights." It is here that he places UNESCO, which he argues "sought to fortify the conceptual connection between literacy and development—and illiteracy and underdevelopment—with its declarations of the Charter of the Book and of 1972 as International Book Year."[12] In this context he directly links UNESCO to the programs for book development of USAID, programs that certainly read the extent of production and consumption of books as a straightforward measure of social and economic development. But while there is certainly truth to his observation that UNESCO was a site of expression of the link between literacy and development, it would be unwise to collapse something like USAID into UNESCO.

For as we have seen, UNESCO was in fact developing its attack on "book hunger" across the years of its greatest divergence from the priorities of the US foreign policy establishment, and many voices within the organization distanced themselves from the US-based mainstream modernization theory that was dominant from the late 1940s through the late 1960s. In Nils Gilman's account, the establishment modernization theorists took modern society to be, roundly, "cosmopolitan, mobile, controlling of the environment, secular, welcoming of change, and characterized by a complex division of labor"; traditional society was, in contrast, "inward looking, inert, passive toward nature, superstitious, fearful of change, and economically simple."[13] Thinkers like Edward Shils, Talcott Parsons, Walter Rostow, and Lucian Pye sought to create a systematic blueprint for modernizing foreign societies, involving a set of inseparable and comprehensive processes, especially "technological advancement, urbanization, rising income, increased literacy, and the amplification of mass media." In 1964, for instance, Rupert Emerson argued that "what makes 'modernization' modern is the ability to live, to think, to produce, to organize, in substantially the same fashion as the Western countries whose imperial hold has now been almost totally broken."[14]

The previous chapter showed how challenges to this dominant policy consensus reached a fever pitch at UNESCO in the 1970s. Pockets of suspicion increasingly plagued the developmentalist ethos. As early as the 1950s, dependency theorists conceived of modernization as an inherently uneven process designed to exploit and deprive the non-Western nations. They argued that it was not a lack of capitalism or any correctable economic stagnation that characterized underdevelopment. Underdevelopment was rather a necessary counterpart to capitalist development in the first world. In the 1960s, radical activists highlighted the lack of consensus even within those nations presenting themselves as the most evolved politically, socially, and economically. Radicals also directly implicated modernization theory in the disaster of the Vietnam War. The global economic and state-legitimacy crises of the early 1970s gave significant impetus to the spreading incredulity toward the idea of endless economic growth. UNESCO became a major platform for this incredulity—a "sounding board for Third-World grievances," as Giovanni Arrighi wrote of the United Nations more broadly.[15]

In UNESCO's *Medium-Term Plan (1977–1982)*, adopted at the United Nations General Conference in Nairobi in 1976, the words "modern" and "modernization" are mostly avoided, and "development" is carefully defined as "an over-all, multidimensional and diversified process essentially endogenous in nature, linked with the values peculiar to each society and requiring the active participation of individuals and groups who are its agents and beneficiaries."[16] The Nairobi plan, which is very much M'Bow's, was described at the time by the *UNESCO Courier* as a "document without precedent in UNESCO's history." It warrants sustained attention here as the most pointed and fulsome articulation of UNESCO's divergence from blueprint modernization.[17]

Primary among the recommendations of the Nairobi plan was that what needed to be accomplished, before any further analysis, was a profound reconsideration of "the phenomena of growth," both in light of the damage to the environment that comes with industrial production and in consideration of the growing inequality that plagues even ostensibly developed sectors of the economy.[18] The plan states that "what is at stake is people's ability to influence their own destiny, to build a significant life and future and to establish creative relationships with others," and it insists that any responsible conception of growth "refers back to something other than itself, for its significance cannot be found merely in its own logic, a logic which would be totally self-contained and would be no more than its own self-justification." What are the effects on individuals of dramatic economic growth, for instance, as consumption "finds itself diverted to the satisfaction of needs which are not essential"?[19] What desires are aroused rather than satisfied by economic growth, and are conducive to alienation in contexts in which people do not feel that they are playing any part in defining or directing the growth process?

The plan defines development as "the full flowering of everything which exists in man in a latent state, the realization of his creativity in all its many forms and aspects" and presents a vision of endogenous development as "summoning up from within the whole spectrum of resources, beginning with the untapped energies and capabilities of the peoples themselves" and taking account of their "specific cultural values and aspirations."[20] In turn, "the conquest of modernity in the Third World countries can be achieved by other means than the passive adoption of a process copied from foreign models."[21] While disparities should be overcome, room must be left for peoples' "particular conceptions of the well-being of the individual and his relations with his fellow men." "Growth," the plan states, "has no meaning unless it contributes to the fulfilment of individuals and of the community, unless it offers greater chances to be human and to create."[22] Echoing here the 1974 United Nations General Assembly declaration and program of action on the establishment of the New International Economic Order, it supports the claim that the quantitative definition of growth via GDP should give way to a concept of integrated development. Through such means, "the work of development" can "become a design for civilization based on truly human values, involving social progress, moral values and the broadest participation in an authentic cultural life."[23] It also gives this vision a historical lineage distinct from European traditions, by drawing upon the particular value accorded to cultural identity at the 1955 Bandung Asian-African Conference and related events in the formation of the nonaligned movement. At the 1960 United Nations General Conference, for example, new member nations from Africa insisted that, while technical aid was important to them, "all development had first and foremost to be rooted in the cultural and social realities of their nations' life."[24]

The 1976 plan firmly links books and other media to this attempt to define forms of development compatible with the sheer multiplicity of cultural identities. It emphasizes, in particular:

> the need vigorously to intensify the efforts to put an end to the imbalance which, as regards capacity to send out and receive information, typifies the relationship between developed and developing countries, by helping the latter to establish and strengthen their own communication and information infrastructures and systems, so as to promote their development, in particular their educational, scientific, technological and cultural development, and their ability to play a full part in the international dissemination of information.[25]

The plan presents the idealization of a free and unimpeded media market as a clear barrier to UNESCO's goals, which must include direct state intervention. It also yokes UNESCO's promotion of books and reading to "the disequilibrium by which the world is confronted at the present time"—a disequilibrium it laments because:

> seeking after values is a cultural process whereby man fashions his essential dignity, his equality with everyone in the world, by communicating, creating, fashioning himself, by giving life a certain meaning and a certain sustainability which stem as much—if not more—from "being" as from "having."[26]

This refusal to distinguish "being" from "having" encapsulates what was at stake in debates about cultural policy and development for UNESCO throughout the early postcolonial period. There could be no distinction between cultural and economic development, as nothing could be achieved if the fundamental inequities in the global distribution of cultural and economic resources were left unresolved. "Having" is not sufficient for "being"; a certain sense of the significance of life outside of "having" must exist. And yet, in turn, "having" is not irrelevant, either; arriving at, articulating, and communicating one's sense of one's fundamental values is impossible without a certain measure of "having."

＊ ＊ ＊

Looking more specifically now at UNESCO's book-related programs and documents, we see that while some did imagine the book as the core technology of a naively defined "progress"—necessary, for instance, to any claim to sophisticated reflection and intellection—just as often its laments about "book hunger" were something quite different. They were a reaction against the dominance of wealthy book producers in the developing countries, and they were an accompaniment to dawning information and communications nationalisms, themselves informed by the kind of rejection of mainstream modernization theory that we find in M'Bow's Nairobi plan.

The 1972 Charter of the Book (further articles include "Everyone has a right to read" and "Books are essential to education"), along with pronouncements attending International Book Year, may appear relatively anodyne, but they were simply the compromised, beseeching public face of a combative body of policy research and debate. What could be less provocative than the image that was used by the almost forty countries that issued stamps to commemorate International Book Year (fig. 2), showing two figures linking arms within the opening of a book? Yet, by what means is such congress to be achieved? Is the image a hectoring reminder of the conditions that don't exist? Is it a dream? It is evident in the research that UNESCO undertook or facilitated during this period that there were seriously conflicting takes within the organization on the desirability and means of attaining modernity as the grounds, or ultimate aim, of cross-border cultural traffic. Also apparent are concerns about the domination of Western corporations and the means of overcoming it, and about the pressures that arise when intellectual and cultural legitimacy is thought to reside in and be bestowed from within the Western nations. A further debate concerned whether one should advocate the "free flow" of books across borders and Western book donation programs, however driven by ideological interests and however indifferent to local circumstances, or whether one should instead promote state regulation of the transnational flow of books, to favor "balance" and encourage indigenous ownership.

It was in 1964 that book production and consumption in the developing world

Figure 2. International Book Year Logo. 1972. UNESCO.

took root as one of UNESCO's signal concerns. At the United Nations General Conference that year, a proposal from Czechoslovakia encouraged UNESCO to embark on a new program of book development focused on the production of low-cost books.[27] A similar proposal put forward a few months earlier at a meeting in Washington, DC, convened by USAID, recommended that UNESCO take on a leadership role in the book development field. A *UNESCO Courier* article states that as of 1964 "the time had now come for UNESCO to make a concerted attack on the central problem of helping to build indigenous publishing capacity in the developing countries."[28] Before 1964, UNESCO had already done some work to encourage the development of the global book trades. It had established a center for the promotion of reading materials in Karachi in 1958 and centers to promote educational publishing in Accra and Yaoundé soon after. It had established model libraries and library training centers in various regional capitals across India and Africa, and by the early 1960s the Collection of Representative Works included two hundred works from forty languages translated into English and French. But it was after 1964, and increasingly over the next decade, that new book development efforts were placed at the heart of UNESCO's mission.

Responsibility for book development was given to one unit within the

UNESCO Secretariat, which served to focus the organization's disparate book-related activities and to instill in the organization a sense that the development of book industries was one of its core concerns. The same Czechoslovakian resolution of 1964, which claimed that books foster "mutual understanding and economic and social development" and called for action to stimulate production of low-priced books for the newly literate, invited René Maheu to present for 1967–1968 a coordinated program "to promote the production and distribution of books in the developing countries."[29] Regional meetings on book development followed in Tokyo in 1966, in Accra in 1968, and in Bogota in 1969. These were followed by a meeting in Cairo in 1972.

The programming that arose from these meetings contrasted quite starkly with UNESCO's earlier book-related efforts. The shift in thinking about the role of the book can be neatly summarized in the growing tendency to slot discussion of book-related programming under the heading "mass media" rather than under "arts and culture"; the first report on the progress of UNESCO's turn toward book development, titled *Books for the Developing Countries*, is number 47 in Reports and Papers on Mass Communication. The Collection of Representative Works had been focused on translation of the world's esteemed literatures into English and French; it was, as we have seen, more about facilitating Western acquisition of knowledge of "other" cultures than about fostering genuine cross-cultural exchange. In contrast, the programming that emerged in the 1960s and 1970s stressed that the lack of indigenous cultural production would not be rectified by this kind of flow of cultural works from the "lesser known" languages into the dominant tongues.

Indeed, whereas UNESCO's original constitution speaks of promoting the "free flow of ideas by word and image" and supporting measures to "give the people of all countries access to the printed and published material produced by any of them," by the 1970s these goals appear to be in conflict. If the flow is "free," will that not ensure the dominance of the already developed industries and thus, in fact, prevent people from accessing materials that do not originate in a few powerful nations? Moreover, is the problem simply one of access to materials or should the focus rather be on the content of what is available, since a failure to support local cultural production may mean a severe limitation on what certain communities are able to communicate about their own experiences, values, and goals?

The research UNESCO supported at this time grappled with precisely these questions. Robert Escarpit's *Révolution du livre*, published in French in 1965 and in English the following year, states that the hunger for books could only be

overcome by "a vast collective effort bringing into play all the scientific, technical, and mechanical resources of the advanced civilizations, by a profound and
systematic reform of social structures, by a concerted world policy which will
affect many other sectors."[30] His later work, *The Book Hunger*, coauthored and
coedited with Ronald Barker, who was then secretary of the UK Publishers Association, speaks of "areas of abundance, areas of scarcity and areas of famine" in
the world of books.[31] *The Book Hunger* opens with the statement that two-thirds
of the world's people "are handicapped in their search for a better and fuller life
by lack of one of the essential tools of progress: books and reading material." It
goes on to state that books are "the simplest and most effective means for the
transfer of knowledge" and laments that "low production, inadequate distribution
channels and the high cost of importing sufficient numbers of books combine
to deprive the public of the reading materials they need." Barker and Escarpit
note that only one of five titles originates in a developing country, and that of
the roughly five hundred thousand titles issued each year, about 80 percent
come from Europe, Japan, the Soviet Union, and the United States. In 1969,
45.4 percent of new titles originated in Europe, while only 13 percent of
the world's population lived there. This is explained by its intellectual influence
and high level of development, but also by the "survival of productive and dis-
tributive mechanisms resulting from its former political supremacy."[32] Barker
and Escarpit note as well that at the meeting of experts on book development in
Accra, it was said that 75 percent of books sold in Africa were imported. They
are clear on the point that the remedy to these imbalances is not to be found
in foreign aid, nor in simply allowing the international trade to continue in its
usual course. Indigenous production is crucial, especially because, echoing the
Charter of the Book, they consider that to write, to publish, and to read should
be "among the inalienable rights of man."[33]

Philip Altbach's UNESCO-backed books and articles make similar claims,
objecting in particular to the ways in which developing nations were dependent
on foreign scholars to interpret their own situations. Objective scholarly inquiry
was, to his mind, stymied by this situation. In an article on "literary colonialism,"
he attributes part of the problem to the copyright regime, which ensures that it is
"difficult and expensive for Third World nations to translate and publish materials
originally appearing in the West."[34] Western firms naturally wanted to remain in
a position to export their own books rather than allow local reprinting. Altbach
argued that international copyright law embodied the dominance of industrial

nations in the world market; it was only changing slowly and without much effect after decolonization. He and Eva-Maria Rathgeber also wrote against the wealthy nations' book donation schemes as a means of rectifying the problem. These donation schemes appeared mainly to flood local markets with inexpensive foreign titles, thus undermining local production, and the contents of the donated books were too often determined by Cold War ideologies.[35]

Likewise, Keith Smith, in work published by UNESCO, opposed the continued domination, in the postcolonial nations, of the metropolitan elite that controlled the book industries. He claimed that the metropolitan and transnational orientation within postcolonial nations meant that local writing struggled not just to find outlets but to find legitimacy, blocked by a "syndrome" of intellectual dependency that is the "outcome of patterns of knowledge-generation and colonial history" and is now "reinforced by elements of world capitalism and intellectual, linguistic, and academic trans-nationalism."[36] He argued as well that "the predominance of metropolitan books combined with other transnational forces has led to the polarisation of intellectuals in LDCs [lesser developed countries] into a larger metropolitan-oriented transnational class and a smaller fervently indigenous protest class." This metropolitan orientation, combined with the transnational orientation of the dominant class, acts as a "powerful control on the legitimising of LDC intellectual writing."[37]

Further UNESCO-backed studies included the aforementioned *Books for the Developing Countries* (1965); *Books for All: A Programme of Action* (1973), which was written to complement and forward International Book Year goals; Altbach's *Publishing in India: An Analysis* (1975); Datus C. Smith Jr's *The Economics of Book Publishing in Developing Countries* (1977); *Roads to Reading* (1979) by Ralph C. Staiger, executive director of the International Reading Association; as well as Anne Pellowski's *Made to Measure: Children's Books in Developing Countries* and S. I. A. Kotei's *The Book Today in Africa*, both published in 1980. Kotei quotes the president of the Ghana Association of Writers, Atukwei Okai, on the implications of an imbalanced system for local writers: "All our best work . . . appears first to an audience which either regards us like some glass-enclosed specimen . . . or like an exotic weed to be sampled and made a conversation piece . . . or else we become some international organization's pet."[38]

So it is with good reason that in their 1980 study of books in the developing world, Altbach and Rathgeber call UNESCO "the most active international agency in the field of publishing."[39] An important consequence of this research activity was that, along with the policy documents and events that the organization backed, the study of the book trade became a crucial accompaniment to the discussions of cultural policy and the highly controversial media policies that UNESCO articulated throughout the 1970s. Most notable among these policies were those associated with the New World Information and Communications Order (NWICO).

The NWICO concept first came about at a 1970 UNESCO conference in which the developing nations, led by India, demanded that the language of "free flow" be replaced by that of balance.[40] This conference was followed by a series of meetings that took place in the developing world from 1972 on. At the 1973 Algiers Conference of the Heads of State of the Non-Aligned Countries, leaders of 75 nations declared that "it is an established fact that the activities of imperialism are not confined solely to the political and economic fields but also cover the cultural and social fields, thus imposing an alien ideological domination over the peoples of the developing world."[41] Meetings of experts from UNESCO and other organizations followed in various locations around the world, involving the preparation of elaborate documents affirming the initial Algiers Programme of Action, which hoped, among other things, to "expedite the process of collective ownership of communication satellites" and "reorganize" "existing communication channels which are the legacy of the colonial past and which have hampered free, direct and fast communication between them."[42]

These proposed actions questioned the supposed impartiality of the news, which was controlled in fact, they maintained, by "profit-seeking private information monopolies" that had zero interest in the needs of poor people and poor nations. Even in the developing world, if indigenous mass media wanted to compete with their foreign peers they had to adopt "market-based institutional structures."[43] The new communications order that was envisioned as an alternative, and imagined as an accompaniment to the broader New International Economic Order discussed at the United Nations, would entail a vast democratization of access to information and to the means of production of information. It would also entail a leveling de-professionalization, in order to place less emphasis on Western-style credentials and production standards, along with an effort to artificially balance media systems so as to favor the development of national industries over foreign content. The only way to accomplish these goals was through new regulatory frameworks, which might be devised by international intergovernmental agencies but would need to be implemented and enforced at a local level, by national governments.

Early versions of the communications policy put forward at these sessions clearly mirrored the logic behind the Charter of the Book and UNESCO statements around International Book Year: for book production, as for general media making, the cost of production meant a hard choice between isolation and dependence on the exports of major corporations, and the doctrine of free flow perpetuated by the dominant economies, like most of the book donation schemes, meant one-way traffic between the dominating and the dominated. Furthermore, these media policy meetings led to the articulation of claims for possible new human rights, like the right to self-interpretation, the right to inform, and the right to be heard.[44] These goals echoed those expressed in UNESCO-backed book development research, which tended to promote cooperation within the developing world in sharing regional resources and in moving together to acquire more; a reordering of tariff rates to benefit local production rather than penalize it; advocacy for creating more space for Third World content in the West; and more state funding to support indigenous authorship and book production.[45] It was as a result of these discussions that UNESCO supported and authored a number of lengthy studies of the communications industries worldwide in the late 1970s.

One crucial example is the 1978 "Declaration on Fundamental Principles Concerning the Contribution of the Mass Media to Strengthening Peace and International Understanding, to the Promotion of Human Rights and to Countering Racialism, Apartheid and Incitement to War." Known popularly as the "Mass Media Declaration," its early drafts were torn apart by British and American representatives and, from another angle, by the Soviet Union, which objected to what it perceived as the prevalence of Western influence. The dominant Western powers were willing to admit that structural imbalances existed in the global distribution of media resources, but they would only explain these as natural market mechanisms that should be corrected through private enterprise, perhaps supported in the short term by one-off Western charity in the form of donations and training programs. State regulation was entirely off the table, much to the chagrin of the Soviet Union, which advocated subordinating the media to the goals of the communist state and society.[46] As a result, to the consternation of key figures like M'Bow, the declaration had to be heavily modified. Any reference to "the rights of peoples" became "human rights" because, in the words of one particularly hostile US commentator, to refer to "the rights of peoples" is to make "individual rights into group interests [and to make] the state their source and arbiter."[47] All references to the responsibilities or duties of the state or media organizations were also eliminated, as was any prescription that the state "should" do something, or even that it was "invited" to do something; these were replaced instead by statements with vague agency, such as: "the mass media contribute to promoting human rights."[48] The document that resulted from these discussions is a revealing barometer of UNESCO's attempt to accommodate deeply divergent viewpoints. Consider, for example, the sixth article of the declaration:

> For the establishment of a new equilibrium and greater reciprocity in the flow of information, which will be conducive to the institution of a just and lasting peace and to the economic and political independence of the developing countries, it is necessary to correct the inequalities in the flow of information to and from developing countries, and between those countries.[49]

Here the reference to the necessity of righting imbalances does not come with any detailed case for how exactly that should occur. The once crucial matter of defining the state's role vis-a-vis the marketplace is entirely obscured.

Even in its diluted form, the Mass Media Declaration was not widely embraced. It was, however, subsequently submitted for consideration to the MacBride Commission, a sixteen-member body created by UNESCO to study communication issues under the leadership of Séan MacBride, the founder of Amnesty International and a holder of Nobel and Lenin prizes for peace. The MacBride Commission in turn produced its own report, which provides further evidence of the compromises involved in the formation and articulation of media policy at this time. It begins, for example, by mentioning "the domination that has been conferred by colonial rule," then modifies that language to suggest that its focus is in fact not domination per se but simply "advantages derived from a faster and earlier process of development."[50] It later cautiously avers that, at "the risk of engendering sharp controversy, it might be said that an essential criterion of freedom of information is diversity of sources, coupled with free access to these sources."[51] This passive formulation, "it might be said," which presents its authors as claiming no power or will to articulate a holistic vision, but rather as reporting on what "could" or "may" or "has" been said, persists throughout. It notes "criticisms formulated in many developing countries" of the one-way information flow and the monopolistic and oligopolistic trends that are "widely discussed in many international instances, gatherings and seminars." It mentions that it is "frequently stated [that] the image of the developing countries is false and distorted," and that this distorted image is sometimes presented to developing countries themselves—or so say the more "vigorous critics."[52] These cautious formulations are clear dilutions of the direct advocacy of state regulation of a balanced media system that had been floated in the early 1970s.

In sum, in the 1960s and 1970s many people working with and for UNESCO were interested in attempting to translate research about underdeveloped book and media industries into specific strategies for reform. Western opposition to this process was highly successful. The debates about the "politicization" of media policy were used as an explanation for the withdrawal of US and British funding from the organization in the 1970s and then the total withdrawal of the United States, Britain, and others in the 1980s. They left after a tightly controlled and orchestrated media campaign against UNESCO, designed to suggest that the organization was taking steps to push "statist" regulation of industry that were akin to socialist or communist practices. Hence my claim that, while some of the member nation representatives to UNESCO during this era would have surely sympathized with the naive and singular vision of development that Joseph Slaughter castigates, the majority seems not to have done so. The problem was precisely that the majority was eventually overpowered by a minority that was more economically powerful and could control the same media of information dissemination that it so loudly claimed should be free. Actually, "control" is not quite the right word here: some Western publishing industry and media advocates regularly lobbied and advised UNESCO representatives. As historical accounts of the period have shown, they became in effect judges of their own case. Their key weapon in fighting media reform—reform aimed at righting the imbalance in access to the means of production of information—was their control over the media itself.[53]

* * *

The book donation programs put together by USAID, the US Information Service, and the British High Commission, to name a few, tell us a lot about what the Western powers *could* tolerate. These were programs designed largely to distribute US and British books overseas, and most research suggests that they actually stifled rather than encouraged local production by, for instance, offering titles at highly subsidized prices and thus driving more expensive local books out of the market. To focus for just a moment on US efforts: they were, and this should be no surprise, designed to promote US interests abroad and to offset the influence of related Soviet programs. A 1960s USAID manual emphasized both the more abstract means of promoting American interests—distributing science and engineering textbooks that might help "develop economically viable democratic societies"—and the more direct means, namely subsidizing the export and purchase of titles that would reflect "the full spectrum of American life and culture."[54]

These programs were developed in lockstep with the massive Soviet book donation schemes in place at this time, which aimed to publicize material progress as the fruit of Soviet communism, to display sympathy for the cultures of the emerging postcolonial states, and to support the image of the Soviet Union as committed to the dissemination of knowledge by distributing free scientific and technical materials. In 1982 the Soviets distributed 74.5 million books in fifty-six non-Soviet languages, including 24.3 million in English.[55] Reaction to the Soviet information offensive shaped how the countering US programs were envisioned and managed, as Trysh Travis has suggested. For example, a 1960s publicity campaign for Books USA, designed to spur public donations and imagining its Soviet equivalent to be little more than propaganda, embraced in contrast the idea of "the power of serious literature to effect personal transformation." The campaign presented the image of an African reader who was less the product of a "communist-inflected nationalism" and more a member of a "thoughtful transnational community of bespectacled booklovers."[56]

In a 1984 report lamenting the decline of US book donation schemes, Curtis Benjamin, an industry consultant and one-time president of McGraw-Hill, perhaps best captures the logic linking the enlightened book reader to the spread of capitalist modernity and promotion of US interests. Benjamin writes that books "cultivate the intellect, the spirit, the creativity, and the innate yearning of every individual for freedom and opportunity to improve his or her way of life and give it more meaning."[57] This lofty tone is not maintained throughout. He soon writes that "to businessmen, industrialists, and financiers, they condition overseas markets and increase exports of US products and services. . . . For most multinational corporations and traders, books serve as invaluable tools for indoctrination and training of the vast indigenous personnel required for overseas operations," while "to engineers, architects, and construction firms, [books] often are precursors to the winning of overseas contracts." Books are great for business, and yet magically they are also, according to Benjamin, the best antidote to the "denigrating propaganda" through which the United States' competitors and detractors castigate it as a "nation of materialistic, money-mad, ruthless 'Yankee Traders' who have little or no regard for the finer things of life."[58]

Exporting books eases commercial exchange but also presents a nation of people motivated by goals higher than commercial exchange. Harmony indeed.

It is important to note once more the difference between this approach and the UNESCO model. Many of the programs UNESCO supported at this time were designed to offset imbalances in the communications system. The political determinants and implications of these activities are complicated. Identifying a "book hunger" was not always about claiming that there was a necessary connection between being a book reader and being a "modern," fully developed human—although sometimes it was. Regardless, the fact that part of the world had an inordinate hold over resources, including intellectual and cultural resources, was never far from view. The pressing realities of the complete disparity in control over communications activated during the colonial period could not be ignored.

What the legal historian Konstantina Tzouvala has argued is partly correct: some of the proponents of the New International Economic Order (NIEO), which the NWICO paralleled, were private business owners in the developing nations who sought preferential trade terms so that they could "catch up" with the developed nations.[59] In the mid-1970s, Immanuel Wallerstein had argued, damningly, that "we do not live in a modernizing world but in a capitalist world" and that the "problem for oppressed strata is not how to communicate within this world but how to overthrow it."[60] NIEO demands did not seem set on overthrowing anything. They included "the absolute right of states to control their natural resources, the establishment and recognition of state-managed resource cartels to stabilise (and raise) commodity prices, the regulation of transnational corporations, technology transfers from North to South, the granting of preferential (nonreciprocal) trade preferences from the Global North to the Global South, and debt forgiveness."[61] Parties to the NIEO tended to accept the views expressed in the original UN charter, that "higher standards of living, full employment, and conditions of economic and social progress and development" are essential to the creation of conditions of well-being and security.[62] The NWICO debates were in their way similar, since the development of communications infrastructure was their apparent goal. That said, like many of UNESCO's studies of books, arguments in favor of a NWICO were occasions for the articulation of important critiques of imperialist media domination and intellectual and cultural dependence. They unearthed the interdependence of economic and intellectual systems and recognized that the book had become a specific kind of tool: a tool controlled by a small part of the world's population and yet needed for participation in a global conversation about what kind of global order would unfold in the wake of colonialism.

It is telling that this conversation was quashed so handily. A powerful minority, protected by an international intellectual property regime that favored producer nations, had a clear interest in ensuring that the developing nations would continue to be net consumers of culture. The withdrawal of the United States and the United Kingdom from UNESCO was financially devastating, and the organization's subsequent policy making certainly suggests that it considered securing their return to be a high priority. The United States continued to threaten to withdraw funds, which hovered at around 25 percent of UNESCO's budget, even after it rejoined in 2003. Recently, in fact, it did indeed again stop payments; it then exited UNESCO completely in response to the organization's having become the first under the UN umbrella to vote to grant membership to Palestine.

The sort of book-historical research that UNESCO had been supporting in the developing world was doomed several times over by the nature of the forces arrayed against it. The organization's suggestions for how to correct industry imbalances were challenged by the nations who stood to benefit from the further solidification of their own productive power, while its credibility as a source of academic research was undermined by models like Darnton's communications circuit, which normalized the kind of stripped-down cultural markets, ostensibly free from any regulatory constraint, that the representatives from the developed nations preferred. Although UNESCO was the most important source and clearinghouse for research on the book trades throughout the 1960s and 1970s, when book history cohered as a discipline in the early 1980s its terms marginalized the approaches that much of the UNESCO-based work involved. More broadly, UNESCO's combative approach to the book was at odds with the new globally dominant political order, which began to take firm hold of the world's governments in the early 1980s. With the establishment of this dominant order, UNESCO's proposed book and media policies advocating state intervention to foster a balanced media system were handily defeated, and its highly politicized and interventionist research on the barriers to book production in the developing world was increasingly sidelined in favor of the kinds of programming that characterize our contemporary moment.

5 Policy Making for the Creative Industries Today

IN RECENT YEARS, UNESCO HAS DEVELOPED rigorous mechanisms for gathering and analyzing data charting the organization's actual effectiveness—real on-the-ground proof that its programs are doing something. It has turned ever more avowedly toward the issuing of "guidelines" and "frameworks" rather than prescriptions. It has embraced market-facing rationales for cultural programming, while stepping up assurances that it is committed to working in the service of capitalist democracy, with freedom of speech and individual human rights trumpeted above anything like collectivization or state control of media and cultural industries. It is not sufficient to explain these claims as a response to the bullying tactics of the wealthier member nations. They reflect instead a world-encompassing trend toward marketized neoliberal governance—governance that itself responds to global conditions of deepening economic crisis.

After the economic turbulence of the 1970s and early 1980s, many of the UN member nations who had been in favor of state intervention to reform the global system were forced by World Bank and International Monetary Fund policies to agree to Structural Adjustment Programs (SAPs) to secure loans. In 1990, the Midnight Notes collective described SAPs as crucial mechanisms for creating "the new enclosures." Processes of "rural impoverishment, dispossession and war have swelled the ranks both of the employed global working class and the global reserve army of labour," David McNally writes. For the first time in history, most people in the world live in urban areas.[1] New forms of the global division of labor have emerged from this transformation. They foster and capitalize on the potential workforce produced by the new enclosures and by the wars and instabilities that attend enclosure and proletarianization. The more affluent economies continue to benefit from and exploit the needs and instabilities of the underdeveloped regions, for instance when a loan conditionality forces the state to seize land to pay debts, or manufacturing is outsourced to regions with the cheapest labor—workers who are also the least able to refuse the most dangerous and toxic jobs. John Smith notes that by 2010, 79 percent of the world's industrial workers were living in underdeveloped regions. The corresponding percentages were 34 percent in 1950 and 53 percent in 1980; meanwhile, in contrast, the percentage of the total industrial workforce that lived in the wealthy countries in 2010 was 21. Echoing the Midnight Notes collective, Smith argues that "uproot[ing] hundreds of millions of workers and farmers in southern nations from their ties to the land and their jobs in protected national industries" has "accelerated the expansion of a vast pool of super-exploitable labor." This increased supply, combined with border controls that suppress the mobility of non-elite workers, has served to produce "a dramatic widening of international wage differentials."[2]

What we have then, Smith argues, is evidence of a new imperialist stage in capitalist development, "where 'imperialism' is defined by its economic essence: the exploitation of southern living labor by northern capitalists."[3] The catching up that the ideologues of development imagined in their heyday has not materialized. On the contrary, there has been a reinforcement and exacerbation of imperializing extraction, which produces and exploits under- and unemployed populations at the peripheries. The processes are global: the capture of dwindling profits by a wealthy elite and the conversion of newly dispossessed populations into absolute surplus or a readily exploitable and expendable labor pool; the movement of people out of agricultural work and into industry; and their simultaneous movement out of industrial work and into the service sector, informal work, underemployment, and joblessness.[4]

* * *

These are the conditions we must keep in mind as we arrive at a third era in the history of UNESCO's cultural policy making, when culture as "resource" begins to take precedence. The nature of that resource, however, is imagined quite differently, with different material effects, according to whether a program targets a relatively wealthy region or one that is plagued by underdevelopment.

To be sure, it is clearly no longer possible for UNESCO to marshal much support for any scheme that involves substantial state-based funding or regulation. The telling exception, described further in the next chapter, is the enforcement of adherence to copyright and intellectual property laws and conformity with protocols set out by the World Intellectual Property Organization (WIPO) and in the General Agreement on Tariffs and Trade (GATT). The realization of UNESCO's perennial commitment to establishing harmony amid diversity is now fundamentally dependent on the existence of viable, legitimate, legally protected markets for cultural import and export. Harmony itself is openly touted as a means of securing the social stability required for capitalist accumulation to continue. All of UNESCO's more recent policy making efforts have been shaped by the requirement that they efficiently, effectively, and observably secure the economic profitability of culture, or at least some measure of its economic protagonism. Culture is generally conceived as a form of wealth that, properly husbanded, protected, and promoted, results in job creation and economic development thanks to growing visitor and creative economies.[5] In order to prove its ongoing value and to avoid having deficit-plagued member nations withdraw or decrease funding, UNESCO must constantly narrate the potential of culture to measurably, demonstrably play a generative economic role. It thus affirms the common intuition that culture's portion of overall economic activity is on the rise. It connects a vibrant cultural infrastructure to the development of a young and dynamic workforce, whether its members are employed in cultural fields or not. Against the model of significant state regulation and control, it affirms the superiority of the development of conditions conducive to the health of private-sector culture. Even the most apparently non-market, noncommercial cultural experience can be put forward as something worth supporting via continued participation in UNESCO activities, in that culture can help people to reconcile themselves to otherwise immiserated or unsettled conditions.

From this common ground, though, there are distinctions to be drawn between the policy work directed at, respectively, the developed and the developing economies. In the developed economies, UNESCO's institutional resources largely tend to support and sustain existing metropolitan markets for culture, where relatively wealthy and leisured consumers are assumed to power the dynamism of the creative economy. In the developing world, in contrast, resources are often solicited from partnering NGOs, foundations, and the private sector and then directed at programs to support new creative enterprises. The hope is that these last will offer much-needed employment opportunities, integrate new economic actors, and ease the social strife and discontent associated with rising rates of superfluity and underemployment.

* * *

The City of Literature program is one of the clearest examples of policy making that targets the developed economies. The International Publishers Association, the International Federation of Library Associations and Institutions, and the International Booksellers Federation back the program. These represent the book industry's three major sectors—publishing, libraries, and bookselling—and they have representatives on the UNESCO nominating committee. The associations collaborate with UNESCO and other stakeholders in the book industries, as well as others within the cities in question, to implement the programs proposed in the application for official designation.

The nomination criteria for Cities of Literature include the quality, quantity, and diversity of editorial initiatives and publishing houses; the quality and quantity of educational programs focusing on domestic or foreign literature in schools, including universities; an urban environment in which literature plays an integral role; experience in hosting literary events and festivals promoting domestic and foreign literature; the existence of libraries, bookstores, and cultural centers that can promote and disseminate domestic and foreign literature; an active effort by the publishing sector to translate literary works; and involvement by the media, including new media, in promoting literature and strengthening the market. Cities of Literature nominated thus far have included Norwich, Edinburgh, Melbourne, Dublin, Iowa City, Reykjavik, Baghdad, Quebec City, and Krakow.

These cities, like those designated World Book Capitals (a sister UNESCO initiative recognizing programming dedicated to books and reading), become part of the Creative Cities network, if they are not already. This is the broad normative framework that serves as an umbrella for much of UNESCO's cultural policy work today, especially in the established markets. A city can participate in the network by demonstrating special success in one of a range of fields: literature, film, music, crafts and folk art, design, media arts, or gastronomy. For a city to be included, it must have substantial evident assets: for example, cultural infrastructure, creative talent, and educational and training facilities. But it must also promise to be an asset to the network. It must have some "added value" for UNESCO itself and be willing to become an ambassador for the Creative Cities network as a whole. In order to get UNESCO backing, the city must also promise an "in-kind, operational, intellectual and financial contribution."[6]

Cities in the network have demonstrated that they have "public and private infrastructure dedicated to the preservation, promotion and dissemination" of the culture in question; related academic research programs; and media that will promote the activities and practices in question. The sector must be economically vital. There should be professional associations, a growing number of jobs, and fiscal policies in place that encourage growth; and there should be evident initiatives that celebrate cultural producers as the very image of energetic innovation.[7]

These schemes thus treat a city's literary heritage and present book industry infrastructure as an occasion to develop the cultural tourism and creative economy sectors. Cities compete with one another for attention and accolades. If a city is selected as a UNESCO City of Literature, it earns the right to use the brand and the UNESCO logo is released to it. The right to use the logo and be featured in UNESCO promotional activities is an affirmation of existing activity and success in these fields; it does nothing, however, to address larger industry imbalances or unevenness. Such concerns are very much of the past. Instead, the literary is now treated largely as a brand that inheres in particular lucrative industries—industries built on the model of developed public institutions and private markets with large-scale production for a sizeable literate public. There is no real space here for ephemeral market literatures, things printed by hand, or minority interests like avant-garde poetry. Those may be fine as curiosities, but they will not on their own earn UNESCO creative-cities branding rights.

These programs naturally reflect and feed into broader transformations in the relationship between cultural policy making and urban governance. UNESCO is an intergovernmental organization funded by state contributions, but these relatively new branding schemes reward highly developed, market-based industries and public-private partnerships. Putting together an application for inclusion in the City of Literature program involves public agencies and cultural officials, mayors and administrators, and often private-sector consultants who are paid by the city to help with the staging of the application. What they stress are the potential benefits to private-sector economic growth that arise from cultural activity. Government involvement is not inconsiderable. City of Literature programming carries on well after the year in which the application is declared successful, and the associated costs are factored into a city's year-to-year cultural budget. Still, the applications for City of Literature designation tend to emphasize the desire to build capacity for partnerships with private firms, which will realize the potential value to be derived from the various ventures. (To mention just the most obvious example, a literary festival is an excellent boost to a city's restaurants and hotels as well as an occasion for cultural tourists to support local theaters and booksellers.)

A comparison of Krakow's application for City of Literature status with that of Dublin reveals additional dimensions and suggests how it has become increasingly necessary for cities to emphasize not just a wealthy literary tradition but also a capacity for the innovative combination of literary resources with other sorts of media production. The Krakow application, which led to its successful designation as a City of Literature in 2013, reiterates UNESCO's constitutive faith that "literature can contribute to the improvement of social cohesion, stimulate economic growth and the development of creative industries, and have a significant impact on intercultural dialogue."[8] The city of Dublin's application, written just as Ireland's economy was being seriously destabilized by the crisis of 2007–2008, says something similar, stressing that Dublin is in fact "poised to play a leading role in the international promotion of literature as a culturally unifying force."[9] The Krakow application highlights stakeholders' awareness of "the need to strengthen and manage its literary capital" (6), such that the Krakow City of Literature (KCL) project was included in the official Culture Development strategy documents for the city of Krakow for the years 2009–2013 and 2014–2020. The application emphasizes the city's interest in building respect for "the Krakow Brand," which, it is hoped, will lead to increased investment in the city, on the part both of private companies and of municipal, regional, and European Union agencies in a position to target Krakow for development. The point is to build on existing wealth, "to strengthen the determined developmental trends leading to the creation of literary capitals in the spirit of artistic, social and intercultural dialogue" (6–7), in recognition that "urban development based on literature and artistic activity is not only possible, but also extremely attractive and beneficial" (7). The Dublin application, similarly, states that the city has been moving steadily away from manufacturing and toward service-sector employment; the former is said to account for 20 percent of employment and the latter for 80 percent. Cultural tourism is counted as a major employer, while people who say they are traveling as cultural tourists spend an average of 25 percent more than other travelers.

Both the Krakow and Dublin applications emphasize the existing wealth that is evidently required for inclusion in the program: an educated workforce, high levels of employment, renowned universities, dozens of active publishing houses, libraries, and other institutions that support reading and reading-related events, festivals, literary prizes, and so on. They are cities with already vast literary resources, boasting what the Dublin application calls "assets and capabilities" that will be harnessed in the ongoing development of Dublin as "the centre of a creative economic region" (9). Both cities' applications also emphasize the potential of literature to help integrate new immigrants, to foster "tolerance" in increasingly multicultural communities by highlighting "migrant voices" and bringing people together for literary events. And both applications mention their willingness to maximize and nurture the UNESCO brand.

Where the Krakow application is unique, however, is in the way in which it registers a declining faith that an emphasis on relatively traditional literary culture and institutions is sufficient. Every application for designation as a UNESCO City of Literature is about profitable industries and employment opportunities in culture and the arts. Like Krakow's, however, the more recent ones are also about efforts to make literature more interesting and accessible to new generations of potential readers; and they emphasize, also, special efforts made to combine literature as a "soft competency" with the "hard competency" of work in more technology-heavy industries (16). The Krakow application states that the city's literary scene "excels in opening up to new forms of literature: e-books, kinetic poetry, e-poetry, city literary games," and mentions Krakow as "the leader in the digitisation of historic literary collections" (7). And indeed, one of the most important ongoing projects connected to the Krakow City of Literature program is ReadPL—a joint initiative supported by Krakow's Festival Office and by Woblink.com, an e-book retailer and platform. It backs the free rental of e-books and audiobooks with the aim of promoting reading via new technologies. The ReadPL project is indicative of what UNESCO now wants to see in City of Literature programming. It combines public and private stakeholders, and it combines technological development and competence with more traditional culture. UNESCO has thus highlighted the project in its coverage of the City of Literature brand and of culture in Krakow.

Krakow's application for City of Literature designation focuses extensively on the city's "unquestionable potential for the development of innovation," especially indicated by the "high ratio of those employed in the R&D sector to the population" and the "high level of outlays of R&D activities" (15–16). In a telling passage, we read that:

> Creativity is becoming the crucial type of economic capital in the local economy which uses human intelligence, knowledge and sensitivity to an ever greater extent. Krakow lives on the creative work of scientists, engineers, artists, filmmakers, musicians, designers and professionals in various fields of knowledge. There are around 50 companies providing services for business processes, which employ

around 20,000 persons in Krakow and its neighbouring areas. Krakow houses the largest cluster of such companies in Poland, accounting for 40 percent of the employees working in this sector. Outsourcing centres provide a full range of services, from IT support to financial, accounting and legal services. The city is also home to enterprises from the high technologies sector and R&D development centres of large corporations. (16)

One would be forgiven for wondering why this passage belongs in a document that boasts of the city's literary offerings. Its language partakes, though, of an assumption common to creative-economy policy making: that a key rationale for the development of a cultured environment is a capacity to appeal to a young, talented, technologically skilled workforce. Along these lines, another initiative tied to the Krakow City of Literature program was the offer of a free cloth shopping bag with the purchase of three books from local bookstores (fig. 3), whether "a brick" or "something thinner." It is a fitting indication of the effort to cultivate local street-level communities of creative consumption among those with enough of an entertainment budget to purchase three books. The assumption is that such people would also be interested in supporting independent businesses and environmental sustainability.

The literary tradition is, here, simply part of a general knowledge economy, where technology and R&D firms, looking to attract and retain employees, recognize that "innovative entertainment products," including literature, and especially new forms of literary experience, appeal to those with higher levels of education and the right kind of cultural vocabulary and competence. The application states that literature is "entering into new and non-obvious relationships with media technologies, becoming a foundation for the development of the creative sector." These non-obvious relationships take several forms: there is the actual combination of skills, with people bringing more traditional humanities educations to bear on work in the engineering, science, and technology sectors; and there is cultural experience and exposure as a "favourable condition" for "the creation of innovative undertakings" (16). The role of literature in the cultural development of Krakow is thus only in part about the existing wealth of businesses and institutions. It is also about literature's place in a generally vibrant cultural environment, energizing work and inspiring innovation, and it is about literature's capacity to be integrated into new media like smartphones and e-readers.

The definition of the literary, and of the literary city, is shifting, in this respect. It is at once about traditional heritage and a multifaceted fount of new innovations. A vibrant literary culture is part of an enriching environment, associated with originality and anti-establishment courage, with freedom of expression and creativity. As such, it is one among many potential attractors for talent working in other creative sectors, including in technology sectors that might not fit our definition of cultural work. Literary writing is material to be featured on new media platforms, and it serves as inspiration for narrative and worldmaking for video games and other "innovative entertainment products" (52) that are poised "at the interface between culture and business" (51).

* * *

Figure 3. Cloth bag to promote *Read Locally!*, an initiative tied to the Krakow UNESCO City of Literature program.

City of Literature programming largely entails investment in already developed creative economies, the idea being that their growth is thereby further secured. Cities that have been brought into the Creative Cities network are supported by the UNESCO brand, with minimal direct funding, as the point is that the industries involved are already lucrative and self-sustaining. But what about literary programming for underdeveloped economies? Is there any legacy of those 1970s efforts to address "book hunger"? In a word: no. When we contrast UNESCO's literary programming with its broader cultural policy work, we see the organization's apparent acceptance of the relative delimitation of access to literary experiences to elites in the developed world, where extensive literary industries already exist and need little formal support. Literature is now produced in a general atmosphere of nervousness about decline. Certainly, in UNESCO policy making, literary reading is treated as a residual rather than an emergent practice. For inclusion in the City of Literature program, the onus is on applicants to prove that they understand the necessity of developing new readerships and new methods for valuing literature by linking it to conventionally nonliterary industries. UNESCO programs that target developing regions, meanwhile, tend not to highlight literary development much at all. These regions generally lack the sort of established literary industries that UNESCO is interested in rewarding, and it is not thought that such development will be forthcoming any time soon. Instead, their future economic development is thought to require other sorts of programming support.

But what sorts, exactly? Here we can consult the 2005 Convention on the Protection and Promotion of the Diversity of Cultural Expressions, as it is still considered to be the standard-setting framework for use by members in their own efforts to protect cultural diversity. It begins by calling diversity a "defining characteristic of humanity" that should be "cherished and preserved for the benefit of all." It suggests that it is cultural diversity that makes for us a "rich and varied world," while living in a varied world "increases the range of choices and nurtures human capacities and values." To sustainably develop "communities, peoples, and nations," this diversity of values must be preserved. It must be at the heart of a "framework of democracy, tolerance, social justice and mutual respect," and it should ground peace and security. Culture is said to be important to social cohesion and to have special potential as a means of enhancing women's status and roles in society. Each of these attributes, however, is, in turn made inseparable from economic priorities.[10]

The Convention recommends that culture be recognized as a "strategic element" in national and international development plans, especially where its development might aid in the eradication of poverty. Culture, whether traditional knowledge or contemporary creative expression, is a source of both intangible and material forms of wealth. In particular, "the knowledge systems of indigenous people" are included as a form of culture, and Convention signatories are asked to "recognize" that such knowledge contributes importantly to sustainable development. This is the language throughout. The Convention "emphasizes" and "reaffirms" and "recognizes" and "takes into account." It is not a set of strictures, but rather a statement of the correct affective relation to culture's ideal potentialities.

The ideals that the Convention expresses are ones that are impossible to realize without the sort of substantial change that the Convention is in no position to legislate. Yet that is precisely the point: UNESCO has become an increasingly indirect support network that explains to the members of its national commissions and the private sector why they should act in a certain way. It is an example of how governance in the cultural sector has come to emphasize and reinforce the supremacy of market-based imperatives, including the imperative for individuals to organize and manage their creative careers with minimal dependence on state-based supports.

The convention "reaffirms" that "freedom of thought, expression and information, as well as diversity of the media, enable cultural expressions to flourish within societies," but in the absence of serious structural reform in the media industries, which would entail vast state intervention and a shift of power away from capitalist media industries, how will such cultural expression flourish, exactly? Media literacy and general education play a key role here: these are not available to most people in the world, which makes the Convention's insistence on "equitable access" seem quixotic. There is a logic that explains this quixotic reaching, however. This logic maintains that every social inequity and ill can be repaired by private actors within the market, and that the role of governance is to provide guidance and language to support new, unhindered, private accumulation. It normalizes the belief that developed markets repair rather than exacerbate or feed off the iniquitous distribution of resources, and it suggests that individuals must commit to taking active roles in nurturing themselves as skilled workers in exciting, dynamic, rising economies.

If the vitality of cultures is manifest in their freedom to create, disseminate, distribute and have access to their own cultural expressions, how is this dissemination to be achieved in the absence of extensive media industries in the underdeveloped world and of transformations that might encourage their emergence? One could imagine, for instance, the potential establishment of more permissive intellectual property regimes, ones that are not designed primarily to preserve the copyrights of developed-world producers. The fact that the Convention has nothing to say about intellectual property rights, with the exception of noting their importance in "sustaining those involved in cultural activity," is telling in this respect. The intellectual property system emerged in the developed world during the heyday of imperialism and serves the interests of its industries. It is designed to reward individuals and the companies that benefit from their work, and it isolates individual innovation as the key to creativity. As the next chapter details further, attempts on the part of UNESCO's developing-world representatives to reform or opt out of the international copyright regime, or even simply to suspend temporarily the requirement that they adhere to its more stringent clauses, have been stridently resisted by the content-producing, copyright-holding nations.

The 2005 Convention insists that cultural activities, goods, and services not be "treated as solely having commercial value." Yet in the absence of any power to address the dominance of commercial imperatives in the cultural field, it is hard to imagine how its vision of fulsome participation in a global conversation about integral human values is not just utopian yearning. The only mention of imbalance is in a clause "noting" that globalization "risks"—as though the threat had not already been made good on—"imbalances between rich and poor countries." Even this mention of risk comes only after the substantial emphasis of the sentence has been placed on all that new information and communications technologies can afford us, including "unprecedented conditions for enhanced interaction between cultures."

What primarily drives the Convention is the assertion of the complementarity of the economic and cultural aspects of development, made in order to encourage the building and strengthening of the cultural industries in developing countries. Article 14, for example, describes:

(i) creating and strengthening cultural production and distribution capacities in developing countries;

(ii) facilitating wider access to the global market and international distribution networks for their cultural activities, goods and services;

(iii) enabling the emergence of viable local and regional markets;

(iv) adopting, where possible, appropriate measures in developed countries with a view to facilitating access to their territory for the cultural activities, goods, and services of developing countries;

[and]

(v) providing support for creative work and facilitating the mobility, to the extent possible, of artists from the developing world.

In order to measure success in achieving these goals, the Convention also devises a new instrument, the Culture for Development Indicators, or CDIS, to chart the extent to which these recommendations are implemented and are successful in helping to develop local industries. A "viable, effective and cost-efficient tool," the CDIS involves "actors" from the public sector, civil society, and academia in the process of data collection and analysis, to foster "intersectoral dialogue" and "build consensus" when decisions are made about culture and development. No cultural policy is complete now without careful consideration of its "flexibility and adaptability," its "multidimensionality," its "capacity-building and policy impact." The CDIS measurement instrument is itself designed not just to enable the collection of statistics that will be used in the construction of future policy, but to maximize the capacity for data collection.

Part of what the CDIS measures is the results achieved by the International Fund for Cultural Diversity (IFCD), the keynote program designed to encourage the implementation of the Convention. UNESCO solicits private- and public-sector and foundation donations to this fund, which aims to foster sustainable development and "poverty reduction" in developing countries through the building of cultural industries. It is, simply put, a scheme to jumpstart digital and creative economies in the developing world and to thereby incorporate new workers into productive economic life. A quick look at the 2014 Fund brochure, which is designed so as to solicit yet more private funding in the form of a desirable "signature partnership with a global corporation and a major media partnership to bring visibility and credibility," provides a sense of what sorts of projects are preferred. The brochure begins by reaffirming the power of culture "to inspire and unite people, . . . to create employment and generate better livelihoods, and . . . to foster transformative change within communities, in cities and countries, and across societies."[11] All of the key terms are here: employment;

social reproduction ("better livelihoods"); management of social inequity ("foster transformative change"). The fund's aim is to create a "dynamic cultural sector" that helps revitalize local economies, and it finances projects that endeavor to create the right kind of "policy environment," as well as those that encourage the right kind of social change and incorporation into the market. In 2014, around 50 percent of the funds went to "develop professional capacity," while 30 percent supported evidence-based policy-making actions.[12]

The IFCD supported a project in Guatemala designed to bring indigenous students into "sync with the digital era," so that they might become "entrepreneurs through digital technologies." Nearly a hundred thousand dollars went to the *Instituto de Relaciones Internacionales e Investigaciones para la Paz* (IRIPAZ), an NGO promoting Guatemala's cultural diversity through audiovisual media. The brochure notes that as a result, "indigenous students were introduced to the digital world and were taught skills in entrepreneurship in the creative audiovisual sector." Two of these students are particularly celebrated because they have since gone on to start their own businesses.[13] Other projects include the creation of a network for creative professionals in the Balkans; professional training in design and arts for women with disabilities in Yaoundé via the Cameroon Art Revolution organization; a project to measure the value of creative cities in Croatia; and support for a National Framework for Cultural Statistics for Mongolia.

Through support for such projects, the IFCD

> builds a steady path to human development by strengthening the entrepreneurial skills of cultural and creative industry actors, by reinforcing the competence of decision makers in effective policy interventions and by enhancing equal participation of various social groups and individuals in creative activities. The IFCD is therefore first and foremost about empowering people—young cultural entrepreneurs, artists, cultural professionals, civil society actors and local, national decision makers—to take ownership of their development processes and shape their own development pathways. The IFCD has been responding to the specific needs of these actors in 43 developing countries: the need to reinforce cultural and creative industries, to develop professional artistic and creative skills and to establish effective and better informed policies.[14]

Much of this rhetoric will be familiar from earlier chapters, though with a crucial difference. The framing of the IFCD fund seems to offer a resolution to the old UNESCO problem, evident since its founding, of how best to help incorporate communities otherwise not participating in economic life. What has changed in more recent years, notably, is that the problem is increasingly imagined to be the very fact of nonparticipation. The policy debates that defined the former period entailed an ambivalent recognition that the nature of incorporation could itself be compromised—indeed, that due to the nature of the global economic system, it could almost never not be compromised and unequal. Now, though, the problem is seen instead as a lack of the fulfillment of potential as human capital, which is to be rectified by a participation imagined as neutrally and freely available, given the right supports. The documents and stories of the IFCD routinely insist that the specificity and particularity of diverse needs will be respected. This is not blueprint modernization, not a single developmentalist teleology. Nothing to worry about. Policy makers will not be the dominant voices but will rather insist on being equal partners in a process designed to guide and exhibit the creativity and ingenuity of others. There is thus none of the ambivalence that we noted in, for instance, Tayeb Salih's story about the doum tree, in which sadness about the loss of tradition and the sheer force of incorporation attends what is presented as an inevitability. For UNESCO today, it is never a matter of imposition, but of working together, creating partnerships. It is a matter not of unequal and potentially harrowing incorporation, but of the fulfillment of potential. It is rare now for the development of dynamic economies to be presented as a source of hardship and strain; instead, this kind of economic dynamism is conceived as the natural goal of human life, the answer to the problems of immiseration, the very site of the realization of a person's abilities, and a form of empowerment that is a credit to their unique difference.

So many facets of UNESCO's recent cultural policy work are thus crystallized in the IFCD. UNESCO mainly tries to operate as a manager of funds that come from elsewhere. There has been an increasing delegation of tasks to the ostensibly nonpolitical private sector and civil society agencies. Substantial and apparently "objective" assessment measures have been developed that chart how effectively programs have embodied the ideals of the Convention and like documents. There are clearly delimited parameters forbidding any sort of appeal to industry regulation or reform, such as nationalization or even just, say, the elimination of tariffs on the import of cultural goods from the developing world. The regulatory state is invoked only as a source of intellectual property legislation and its enforcement.

Economic development is presented as a wholly positive process that is neutrally available to talented, ambitious, entrepreneurial young people.

We have seen that culture, especially the feeling of affective identification with a national or regional cultural heritage grounding one's sense of self, is supposed to help to ease the strain of living in immiserated conditions. In a 2013 speech, Irina Bokova, as UNESCO's director general, called culture "a wellspring for social resilience" in the aftermath of the 2008 economic crisis and a "source of identity and cohesion" that helped people to deal with "bewildering change."[15] Development itself is never understood as the source of the unwanted change whose physical effects need mitigating, however. Instead, culture-led development, the development of culture as a resource, is the eternal solution.

* * *

Zakes Mda's celebrated novel, *The Heart of Redness*, published in 2000, belongs to the intellectual formation that justifies contemporary cultural policy making. Its narrative crystallizes the faith that cultural industries are themselves a form of humanized economic development. It also contains some of the same wishful thinking about government largess, and about using culture to solve problems of maldistribution of wealth, that subtends UNESCO programs.

Before writing *The Heart of Redness*, Mda had worked in cultural development, and he continues to do so now. He was a cultural affairs specialist at the American Cultural Center in Lesotho—an extension of the United States embassy there. He also worked for the Lesotho National Broadcasting Corporation, and served as director of the Screenwriters' Institute, where he helped to develop materials in development communications. He wrote a PhD thesis and then a book on the use of the theater for development communications. He also produced his own plays, to be staged collectively within the milieu of development theater, and was director of the Marotholi Travelling Theatre company—experiences that he discusses in his scholarship.

The Heart of Redness is a fictional rendering of this substantial history of work and research; it testifies to Mda's expertise in development and communications and his aptitude for cultural policy making. The protagonist, Camagu, is an educated consultant committed to a postcolonial modernity and a humanized form of developmentalism. He has an American doctoral degree and has worked for an international development agency in New York. He returns to South Africa in 1994, after thirty years abroad, hoping to "contribute to the development of his country."[16]

Camagu has already worked as a consultant for UNESCO, for the Food and Agricultural Organization, and for the International Telecommunications Union, but he struggles to find a good job in a South African milieu dominated by a small networked elite. Described as one of the "learned rejects of this new society" (28), he has no clear course ahead of him. Having been captivated by a woman singing at a wake, he decides on a whim to search for her in the seaside town of Qolorha, known to those in Johannesburg as a "wild" coastal outpost that is closer to original Xhosa culture than the denuded cities.

In Qolorha, Camagu is drawn into a conflict with its roots in colonial history and the historic cattle killing of 1857, dividing those known as the Believers from their Unbeliever kin. The novel shifts between accounts of that time and of the present. The Believers are descendants of people who, hoping to restore their original wealth, have put their faith in a prophecy that has counseled them to slaughter their cattle. Having suffered through drought and diseased livestock, they hope that if they kill their cattle now, their food supply will be restored to plenty, with new cattle and generations of ancestors emerging from the sea to form a paradise on earth. The Unbelievers reject the prophecy; some even come to believe that it is a ploy on the part of colonizing Europeans, who want people to be starving and desperate for work so that they will abandon their land and be forced to pay rent to other landowners or undertake waged work in the towns.

This divide fractures the community of Qolorha, where the prophetess Nongqawuse once resided and where her followers would congregate. It determines their disposition toward the village's economic development. Believers, led by Zim and his daughter Qukezwa, stand against a proposed scheme to develop the town into a casino and resort aimed at thrill-seeking tourists. They are wary of the argument that the development will produce jobs for local people. The Unbelievers, led by Bhanco and his daughter Xoliswa Ximiya, promote the scheme. John Dalton sides with the Believers. He is a local hotelier and shop owner whose ancestor fought on the side of the colonists and even shrunk the head of one of Zim and Bhanco's ancestors, but the villagers find him largely tolerable, and even joke that he is more local than the locals. He has an interest in opposing the development scheme in that he is the person who currently benefits most from the small local tourism trade that already exists. Through his small hotel, The Blue Flamingo, he takes tourists to visit a famous site associated with Nongqawuse's prophecies. He also takes them to visit local homes, where he is comfortable paying villagers to dress up in ceremonial clothing while doing menial tasks like scrubbing the floor. Camagu accuses Dalton of selling fake cultural experiences to tourists who do not know any better, while Xoliswa Ximiya, who has recently been made school principal, finds it shameful that any of the local heritage is preserved at all. She is embarrassed by anything associated with "redness," a word she uses only pejoratively, referring to "the red people who have not yet seen the light of civilisation" (261). She is in favor of the town being totally developed via the tourist resort, which promises water sports, gambling, and roller coasters, not least because she wants to see any remaining "redness" eliminated. The Believers, meanwhile, supported by Camagu and Dalton, point out that these amusements will not be available to the local community, who can hope at best for a few jobs. They wager that the community will be giving up more than it gains if it allows the development to take place.

The answer, though, is not simply to keep things as they are. Everyone agrees that some form of economic development is a good thing, and they are experimenting with schemes for indoor plumbing and electricity. It is just a question of which kind of development. This is where Camagu is essential. With his American PhD and his eagerness to help build the country post-apartheid, he has been failed by the city and the hollowness of the "black empowerment" discourse he encountered there, which disguised how few people were experiencing anything like substantial uplift. What he finds in Qolorha is a solution to his personal rootlessness—a way to access those parts of his heritage that he wants to hold onto. He also finds a meaningful way to participate in national development, by saving Qolorha from the proposed development scheme. He lobbies to have the town turned into a national heritage site, and he fosters the expansion of the existing tourism infrastructure, which is largely directed at ecotourists attracted to the beauty of the local area, to its unique trees and birds and the stunning coastline. Camagu wants to preserve rather than transform the existing landscape, to sell the town as a destination for the right kind of visitor: "There are many people out there who enjoy communing with unspoilt nature," he states (232). He also strongly advocates that the business be a cooperative cottage industry that employees own in common and benefit from equally. In other words, they would be self-employed and self-reliant, not working for anyone. His view is that people will not care about any scheme that they have not helped to implement: "They should be active participants in the conception of the project, the raising funds for it, in constructing it," he tells Dalton (207).

Despite their disagreements, he is helped in his pursuit by Dalton, who is the person who ultimately manages a successful application to the Department of

Arts, Culture and Heritage to have the town designated as a preserved national heritage site. The state is a rational and sympathetic force here; it plays an important role in the plot of the novel but is scarcely figured and slightly fantastical. It seems that, even though the government had initially supported the proposed scheme to turn the town into an amusement park and leisure palace, its appreciation for sites of national heritage significance is substantial enough that it will grant a change of course, secured by the partnership between a local white business owner and a black South African with a foreign PhD. Again, when it comes to heritage culture, Camagu is against any sort of performance of traditional culture; he sees it as pandering and exoticizing, and as basically false in that it gives tourists the impression that the local community is something that it isn't—that is, still mired in the "redness" that so irritates Xoliswa Ximiya. He tells Dalton: "It is an attempt to preserve folks ways . . . to reinvent culture. When you excavate a buried precolonial identity of these people . . . a precolonial authenticity that is lost . . . are you suggesting that they currently have no culture . . . that they live in a cultural vacuum?" (286) The industry that he supports instead is merely a minor extension of the cooperative he has already formed with NoGiant and MamCirha, two women who make their living gathering shellfish. He helps them fish and distribute their catch, and soon adds to this the manufacture of traditional Xhosa costumes and accessories, which are trending in Johannesburg, "popular among the glitterati and sundry celebrities of the city of gold since the advent of the African renaissance movement" (185).

Camagu only embraces heritage culture if it is properly historicized and put into a context. He is committed to cooperative community-led development and to the recognition of the inevitable modernity of tradition, believing that nothing of the past can be truly preserved without mediation. He appears to side with the Believers, even eventually marrying Qukezwa, who is associated throughout with the preservation of the beauty, "wildness," and tradition of the place, and severing his romantic attachment to Xoliswa Ximiya. Yet his real commitment is to a secular, non-salvific conception of history and national progress in which tradition can ground personal self-development, but only to a point. This conception is postcolonialist, materialist, and teleological, with development figured as inevitable and welcome if it is managed by authentic community involvement and oversight. Hence, while he does not believe that the prophecies that led to the cattle killing were true, he counsels sympathy for the Believers, because their faith was the product of their destitution. It "arose out of the spiritual and material anguish of the amaXhosa nation" (283). They were being unsettled by colonial forces, their cattle were becoming sick with diseases brought from overseas; they were seeing their primary sovereignty threatened. In Camagu's interpretation, this made them vulnerable to those who asked them to put their faith in prophetic figures who promised to save them and return them to their previous stature. The cattle killing, which served not to offset but to exacerbate the ongoing destitution of the area, was a signal force of primitive accumulation. People left their land, starving, searching for food, and found themselves paupers dependent on colonial largess for work, wages, rented land, sustenance: "Those amaXhosa who continued to occupy their homesteads suddenly discovered that they were squatters on their own land and now had to work for new masters" (296). Many of the novel's historical passages suggest the close alignment between Camagu's and Mda's takes. We read for instance that Sir George Grey, whom locals called The Man Who Named Ten Rivers, had always intended "to break the independence of the amaXhosa by destroying the powers of the chiefs, and forcing their subjects from their land to work for white settlers on their farms and in their towns." Thanks to the cattle killing, he was simply "achieving this sooner than he expected" (296).

Keeping this understanding of the village's history in mind, Camagu's interest is in rejecting the imposed developmentalism that he thinks would be another step toward further destitution. It would cause the local people to give up the possibility of a measure of self-sufficiency and self-government, they would no longer own the land taken over by the company that owned the resort, and they would be forced to try to find work in the tourism industry in order to survive: "The sea will no longer belong to you. You will have to pay to use it" (232), he tells them. He thinks to himself, "Of course, a small number of jobs is better than no jobs at all. But if they are bought at the expense of the freedom to enjoy the sea and its bountiful harvests and the woods and the birds and the monkeys . . . then those few jobs are not really worth it" (118). Camagu's alternative scheme keeps the community from this fate while also attempting to prevent the further museumization of fake-authentic African life. Recall that Dalton's ancestor had helped to capture and kill the father of Twin and Twin-Twin, who are the ancestors, respectively, of Zim and Bhanco. Twin and Twin-Twin discover their father's captors busily shrinking his head in a pot, the skull to be sent back to England where it will end up in a museum; "The heads of our ancestors are all over Europe . . . trophies collected in military action and in executions," Camagu advises learnedly (194). Many of Qolorha's people know something of this history, so they are wary of the way in which they can be subject to the gaze of white Europeans; at community gatherings, they discuss shrunken heads, pilfered wealth, and the display of Saartjie Baartman's genitals. The inclusion of the reference to these colonial practices of display serves to further endorse Camagu's alternative: locally directed, responsive, respectful, careful, historically nuanced development designed to preserve the beauty of the place and benefit the local community first and foremost. What this comprises specifically is a backpackers' hostel that mutates into a "holiday camp": "Tourists are attracted to the gigantic wild fig tree and the amahobohobo weaverbirds that have built a hanging city on its branches" (314). There is also, surprisingly, a cooperative cultural village backed by Dalton, where "village actors walk around in various isiXhosa costumes" (315) in order to "show various aspects of the people's culture in one place" (285).

Though Camagu had strongly resisted having anyone act like something they are not, claiming for instance that the "amaXhosa people are not a museum piece . . . their culture is dynamic" (286), he is not a megalomaniac or dictatorial figure. He is willing to compromise with Dalton. Dalton had after all been instrumental in securing the town's official national heritage status, and there are local villagers who are willing to participate in Dalton's performances, so, Camagu asks himself, who is he to judge? Camagu's undogmatic acceptance of Dalton's ongoing involvement, and his concession that Dalton has lived in the area his whole life and has already worked to develop tourist traffic there, is crucial to the characterization of Camagu. He is respectfully conscious of the fact that he is an outsider who has spent most of his life outside of South Africa and has reached a level of education that makes him unlike the other villagers. He is willing to admit that some concession to the interests of tourists is necessary to ground a fledgling trade. The emphases on ecology and heritage are able to complement each other in order to produce a general tourist infrastructure. We are, in this way, offered a comic fantasy of harmonious reconciliation in which tradition and modernity, humanity and economic development, can coexist and even complement one another.

A few years after *The Heart of Redness* was published, Mda himself financed the founding of the Lower Telle Beekeepers Collective Trust, collecting and bottling honey from an ancestral site in the Eastern Cape. Camagu's community-run tourism businesses and Mda's honey production cooperative are similar in their commitment to cooperative enterprise and to locally attuned developmentalism, the kind that UNESCO would roundly endorse as the best route to a general humanized cultural development that is responsive to, but not held back by, the history of colonial subjection and dependency. In his 1993 book, *When People Play People*, Mda (anticipating his representation of Camagu) writes that the foreign development aid that flowed into Lesotho from Britain and South Africa after independence failed because of an implicit politics: "people did not work together, but instead worked for the aid agency or government ministry as day labourers, paid either with food or with cash." Those who ended up benefiting from development weren't the rural people in the targeted areas, but rather people in the towns, "where offices and houses and infrastructure suited to the needs of donor and local bureaucracies were built, where machines were stored and repaired, and where shops, banks and post offices provided additional support for the elite."

Mda laments that the "recipients of the schemes were treated like immature children" and that the plans for various schemes were "never shown to rural people, much less prepared by them"; planning was instead always "top-down and one-way." It is all but inevitable, then, that people "lack the motivation to participate in the projects of which they feel they are not part" and "see themselves as mere recipients—an attitude which reinforces dependency."[17] Though the action shifts from Lesotho to a rural South African village, the dynamics of wealthy core and impoverished periphery are similar, with wealthy urban South Africa relating to relatively impoverished Lesotho and South Africa's own coastal outposts in similarly dominative and incorporative ways. These dynamics are what Camagu's cottage industries and Mda's beekeeping collective are designed to correct, with their emphases on collaborative planning, collective ownership, self-reliance, and self-employment. This is what Camagu promotes in the village of Qolorha; and indeed, when he has occasion to speak in front of the villagers he takes on the role that Mda promotes for participatory theater development and ideally for a broader mass media: he "conscientizes" the periphery, in the hopes that it will develop the capacity to express its own needs and arrive at its own informed solution to local problems.

*   *   *

A novel like *A Heart of Redness* knowingly plays a different role than does local participatory theater. It assumes an educated international audience and sets out to explain and perhaps justify, in a self-fashioning way, the mentality of those who commit themselves to "conscientizing" local peoples. Rejecting as crassly touristic any kind of participation in exoticization, or the granting of access to faked authenticities, it instead expresses the contemporary cultural-policy mind-set. That is, it explores the consciousness of the cultural worker who conceives the traveling theater company, the cultural development plan, the communications policy that might help local people "analyse their situation" and motivate its transformation.[18] Literature is thus imagined not as itself transformative, but as a supporting plank—an historically responsive, nuanced, respectful support—in the development of a global cultural policy milieu whose strategies of governance are affectively compelling, persuasive, and consented to. This policy milieu is counseled to be supportive, ideally, not of mainstream modernization and whole-sale top-down development but rather of black self-determination and collective activity toward economic growth. Culture-based development is presented as a solution to pressing problems of economic inactivity caused by a lack of invest-ment—both affective and financial.

This understanding of how development should take place is one that UNESCO has largely embraced, and the treatment of literature as at best a type of elite instruction in the ideal affect for policy makers is also evident in UNESCO programming. Mda's faith in culture-based development as a conduit to human-ized economic growth is relatively new, and correlates well with developments like the City of Literature and the International Fund for Cultural Diversity. Literature is one potential site of training in the correct mentality, while other kinds of cultural programming provide the keys to general uplift. Like Mda's novel, UNESCO's recent cultural policy making, which is, by and large, invested in the development of creative industries, is at the same time, in that work, at-tuned to and constrained by the realities of ongoing underdevelopment. The creative-industries imaginary is after all less a reflection of some fantasized, infinitely renewable, postindustrial knowledge economy than it is a strategy by which contemporary governments, plagued by debts and by jobless populations, show their commitment to whatever meager private-sector development they can facilitate.

We also see evidence of decline in a minor way in the literary field even in the developed economies, where "healthy" incorporative labor markets, the expecta-tion of secure full-time work with reliable leisure time, and the healthy tax base that bankrolled the inculcation of the literary disposition and other high-culture dispositions, all now seem to be weakening. So much so that cultural policy making aimed at the continued vitality of the literary field tends to assume a dwindling, aging readership. Supported programs are expected to include some plan for the development of literary experiences that might incorporate new audiences, or to identify new ways of extracting value from the literary tradition, such as via partnerships with the video game or smartphone industries.

Decline is even more relevant, and in a different way, to cultural policy that is aimed at underdeveloped economies. One indicator of the overall lack of dynamism in the global economy—and yet surely not one of the more commonly referenced!—is the fact that literary programming targeting the developing world is by now quite minimal. There has been a deepening of the structural asymmetries that make populations in the developing nations into either attractive cheap labor or a surplus population pushed to the margins of economic life, and UNESCO's unenviable position is to try to encourage the building of creative economies upon the foundation of this wreckage. Even the few good jobs that might arise in new creative sectors are a topical treatment applied to a deep wound. Nevertheless, affective investment in participation in productive economic life is what much UNESCO cultural policy making now attempts to secure. As in Mda's novel, culture is imagined both as a conduit to the right affect and as a source of potentially generative economic activity, while a positive attitude toward official economic activity is the right affect, and the right affect of positivity is the necessary condition for development, and so on ad infinitum.

6 Pirates and Pipe Dreams

UNESCO'S INTERNATIONAL FUND FOR CULTURAL DIVERSITY (IFCD) has on rare occasions supported book-related projects, in contexts in which local book industry development can be presented as a measurable facet of the cultural and creative industries. A recent instance of such funding neatly encapsulates the unique nature of contemporary formations of cultural policy.

In 2013, the IFCD awarded a grant of $93,000 to the Reproduction Rights Organization of Zimbabwe (ZIMCOPY), a nonprofit organization "committed to the promotion of the respect for copyright in Zimbabwe." The grant was to enable ZIMCOPY to develop, with UNESCO's help, "a national strategy to strengthen the enforcement of copyright law in Zimbabwe" and to create as well "a platform to regularly review this strategy." A UNESCO profile of the project, written to coincide with and promote World Book and Copyright Day in 2017, calls it "exactly the sort of project that the IFCD supports," because it "aimed to shore up a facet of Zimbabwe's cultural industry."[1]

We saw in the last chapter that the IFCD aims to build creative industries in developing countries. It does so by channeling funding to private-sector cultural producers or to projects that combine public, quasi-public and private partners, so long as their goals include the generation of activity in the private sector. The ZIMCOPY application was supported by the idea that book pirates are impeding the development and economic health of the book sector in Zimbabwe.[2] In project coverage, these pirates are said to have "taken" more than half of the market share away from "legitimate publishing business," with the dramatic result of leading "authors to simply not feel like writing books anymore."[3] The ZIMCOPY organization is thus positioned as stepping in to defend the interests of local writers who can otherwise no longer find motivation to work. UNESCO's profile of the project states that Zimbabwe otherwise has a vibrant literary scene, including prestigious festivals like the Zimbabwe International Book Fair. It also mentions the fact that Zimbabwean authors are often entered into the competition for the Caine Prize for African Writing, while recent "success stories include NoViolet Bulawayo's *We Need New Names* or Bryony Rheam's *This September Sun*," which have "stimulated an interest in local literature."[4] Mentioning these examples of relatively famous authors here positions ZIMCOPY as their champion. Without its protection and advocacy, piracy will continue to run rampant, and those who aspire to high-stature careers may not be able to do much more than eke out a meager living, if they even care to bother.

Yet the occurrence of piracy might also be understood differently, as a reflection of the fact that those Zimbabweans who want to read are poorly served by local publishers, who are themselves working under considerable constraints. The readers cannot afford the books sold by legitimate publishers. They cannot or do not wish to shop in the nicer bookshops in upscale malls, but look instead to street market stalls, where pirated copies appear. They share books among their family and friends. They are not particularly worried about the source of the book, so long as they can partake of this portable pastime.

The experiences of such readers suggest that the underdevelopment of the local book industries is far more complicated than the ZIMCOPY mandate would suggest, in ways that make their claims to be protecting local writers like Bulawayo and Rheams somewhat questionable. These are authors who likely could not make a significant income from book sales in Zimbabwe alone. Piracy, far from being the most significant cause of this situation, is most likely better understood as being itself a manifestation of the same forces that make writers seeking literary success look abroad for their audience. These writers may get a start in local scenes and manage to be networked with a relatively successful and high-prestige coterie of African literary professionals. Still, the path for writers who aspire to make a living by writing usually tends to include finding a readership in Europe and North America, where a conventional literary sensibility is more appreciably cultivated and available, and some people are still able to pay high prices for literary books. In this way, writers like Bulawayo are not, in fact, dependent on viable literary readerships in Africa or viably capitalized production facilities there.

The details of the situation for English-language publishers across Africa are relevant here. The post-independence quest to develop literary readerships and publishing and printing trades met with massive hurdles. It was nearly entirely stopped by imposed Structural Adjustment Programs (SAPs) and trade liberalization in the 1990s, and in some countries has now been all but abandoned.

The development of local industry has been stymied by the ongoing global unevenness in the development of media production, and by the fact that there are not the numbers of leisured, highly literate readers with disposable incomes to support the capitalization of a large professional "legitimate" book trade, especially for literary books.

The field of contemporary Anglophone African literature relies on private donors, mainly but not exclusively British or American, supporting a transnational coterie of editors, writers, prize judges, event organizers, and workshop instructors. The literary works that arise from this milieu are normally targeted, understandably, at British and American markets. The Caine Prize itself, which the ZIMCOPY story mentions as a sign of Zimbabwean literary prestige, is adjudicated and headquartered in London, trademarked in the United Kingdom, and funded by the Oppenheimer Memorial Trust, which was founded on money that Ernest Oppenheimer made from gold and diamond mining in Africa. The colonizing nations built their own governments, their "free" public education systems, their "free" public libraries, their social policy and welfare provisions, through taxation of the kind of private wealth that comes with extensive colonial operations and industrial and urban development. We rarely think about the fact that the development of a highly literate reading class interested in getting most of what it needs via legitimate sources—legally operating bookstores, libraries, the school system—is an affordance of advanced capitalist wealth.

Looking at the history of publishing in Africa, Walter Bgoya and Mary Jay, who have made their careers in the African book industries, write that in the early years of independence, only 9 percent of the African population was literate. However:

> With the growth of literacy after independence, publishing developed; predominantly educational publishing by foreign-owned companies keen to develop an untapped market. Books were not originated within Africa, but from publishing decisions made in the north: ideas, writers, and decisions were not African. Even where they were originated by local branches of foreign companies publishing in European languages, it was the parent companies overseas and not the local branches that had the final decisions on their publication.[5]

In her work on the copyright debates facilitated by UNESCO in the 1960s, Eva Hemmungs Wirtén writes that in Africa, when those discussions started, there were "six titles per million inhabitants, only 20 of the 34 countries in the region producing books at all, and a per capita of one-thirtieth of one book per person per year."[6] Nevertheless, while African book production did not appear to be particularly considerable, it remained an important territory for overseas firms that saw potential for growth. They had already made arrangements that favored their continued involvement in local book production. Europe's colonial holdings were automatically included in the internationally applicable Berne copyright convention, and then there was also the Traditional Market Agreement, which was put in place formally in 1947 but merely reflected existing practice. Signatories to this agreement, through which British publishers secured control over markets for English books in what they called their "traditional markets" (some seventy countries), did not give up any publication or distribution rights to American publishers. The agreement had the effect of dividing up global English-language book markets between Britain and the United States—a dominance that continues even now, long after the Traditional Market Agreement was abandoned in the 1970s.

Hence, after independence, rather than developing local industries, state-based agencies like the East African Literature Bureau devised textbooks that were produced by foreign publishers. Supported by government contributions, the Bureau in effect shouldered all the risk on behalf of commercial publishers. It was an attractive deal for the private firms who operated in Africa on this basis.[7] They invested little, if any, of the profit they made within Africa.

In the 1970s and early 1980s, parastatal and independent indigenous African publishing houses were established. However, the African governments, by now preoccupied mostly with economic development and unfolding crises, gave them little or no support, "interpreting culture primarily as folklore and dancing to entertain government and political party leaders or visiting dignitaries," as Bgoya and Jay write.[8] Authors and publishers were not protected by enforced, robust intellectual property law. Piracy was common. As we saw in chapter 4, international book donations stymied local production by flooding the market with cheap or free books. Material costs remained high. Many governments did not see books as exceptionally important to national development, either. They refused to relax duties and taxes on what was needed for manufacture, and the high cost of materials such as paper, ink, and printing machinery made it hard for publishers to sell cheap books. In this environment, the only kind of local book production that governments directly supported was their own state-run textbook manufacture.

The SAPs put in place in the 1980s and 1990s made the existing problems worse.[9] It became even harder for any prospective firm to access financing, with up to 40 percent interest on bank loans and overdrafts. Already impoverished populations had even less to spend on nonessential items. Low literacy continued, especially in the nonindigenous languages in which books were mainly published. Distribution systems were further weakened; already dramatically underfunded, public libraries all but collapsed. Parastatal, university, and independent indigenous publishing were basically all on their last legs. Only foreign publishing houses, particularly British ones, which continued to supply books to tertiary-level institutions and universities, still made some money despite the crisis.

NGOs and private foreign foundations picked up a bit of the slack. The African Books Collective (ABC), which Bgoya headed, was a group of seventeen active publishers in sub-Saharan Africa. They first met in London in 1985 to discuss how to overcome the many hurdles that were impeding significant expansion. The preliminary meeting was funded by the Swedish International Development Cooperation Agency (SIDA) and built on a conference organized by the Dag Hammarskjöld Foundation in 1984, "The Development of Autonomous Publishing in Africa." ABC's start-up capital came from three donors: SIDA, the Ford Foundation, and the Norwegian Agency for Development Cooperation (NORAD). ABC-affiliated publishers struggled to sell titles internationally, due to the constraints of foreign exchange, expensive postage, and the impossible expense of effective international marketing. ABC was thus established in the United Kingdom, from where they marketed and distributed English-language titles worldwide, and donor support used for outward-facing literary production rather than for the development of a local African literary readership.

In an account of her work with Zimbabwe's Weaver Press, Irene Staunton notes that in the immediate postcolonial period, the state and British publishers worked together to develop a flourishing textbook industry. Through the 1980s, a primary school textbook might be printed in a run of upwards of a hundred and twenty thousand copies, and a secondary textbook in thirty thousand. It soon became apparent, though, that the economy was not going to be dynamic enough to support universal public education.

Staunton points out that, to employ the growing numbers of graduates, the economy would have had to grow at an annual rate of 12 percent. Moreover, there was no substantially supported public library service—stock, salaries, and facilities maintenance are costly—and school libraries fared little better. In a country where the formal unemployment rate is over 85 percent, people cannot generally afford books. Those books that do sell moderately well "bring you closer to God, to money (self-help books are popular) and to passing an examination."[10] This is not a context in which small publishers can thrive, and to focus specifically on the literary niche would be basically impossible.

Nevertheless, Staunton claims, "writer" is a status to which many aspire. Weaver Press turns down many manuscripts, and Staunton is struck by the number of writers who confess that they do not themselves read literature. Perhaps they have heard about, or joined, the Budding Writers Association of Zimbabwe or the Zimbabwe Women Writers organization. These are donor funded; they host workshops, publish donor-subsidized anthologies, and have offered space to people who want to write. Donors are thus clearly essential, in a situation in which people want occasions to write and to see their work in print but find impediments to doing much reading and so cannot form part of a purchasing reading community sustaining a viable industry.[11]

In Zimbabwe during the 1980s and early 1990s, new writers' associations and workshops were complemented by the Zimbabwe International Book Fair, which partnered with ABC and the African Publishers Network and was for a while quite a vibrant hub of literary activity in Africa. In more recent years, however, following the turmoil and reforms that have been inescapable since the 1990s, most of this activity has subsided. At Weaver Press, most income has come from having titles prescribed in schools. Until the early 1990s, Staunton writes, "an A level title would sell around 30,000 copies during the three- or four-year period of prescription and an O level title considerably more." Now, however, Weaver Press "would consider ourselves very fortunate to sell a tenth of this number." Why is this? Because, as is true nearly everywhere, the number of students wanting to study literature has declined. Students report that literary books are hard to relate to; pressure on teachers to cover subjects with clear parameters and learning outcomes has grown; and "students don't want to take a subject that has no obvious career path."[12] They are more likely to enroll in business courses.

Staunton is understandably struck by the fact that people seem to aspire more to write than to read. Perhaps, though, the aspiration to write can be explained as a reflection of the unique situation of the local literary scene. It may reflect both a deep desire for self-articulation and expression and an aspirational identification with a career trajectory that is at least moderately upwardly mobile. To be recognized as a talented writer is to come closer to insertion into a potentially sustaining creative writing establishment backed by NGOs and foundations and closer to belonging to a community of young creative producers, whose vitality and interest in evident in the culture of festivals and in the official idealization of the creative economy. To aspire to write, in short, is to aspire to a level of material stability—however modest.

In Staunton's experience, then, Weaver Press "functions more as a non-profit" than as a commercial publishing house.[13] Nor does the future for literary publishers look very bright, in her estimation. It will be donor-supported nonprofit work, not market-facing publishing, given that there is little or no for-profit future. More recent research suggests, in addition, that the form of the physical book has been, and will continue to be, of decreasing importance.[14] Moreover, while direct donor aid from nongovernment sources, usually international, has stepped in to fill some of the gaps left in the wake of state-based support, that aid has been relatively modest and precarious. It has also supported bringing African books to international readers, instead of developing local markets, which is assumed to be a lost cause given the population's overall levels of wealth, English-language literacy, and interest in literature.

To say that a stringent copyright regime has never done much to mitigate this general situation is quite an understatement. Indeed, in Wirtén's terms, "international copyright relations have always been inscribed within a colonial grid."[15] It is tempting to argue that any activity against piracy simply makes books even harder to access—a point of consequence if access to reading material, and not protection of publishers' profits, is your goal. Those in favor of copyright enforcement would deny that these can be separated, however. Their idea is that Zimbabwe's subscription to standard copyright terms and participation in international copyright conventions will help develop the local industry by ensuring that "legitimate" legal publishers earn sufficient profits. Yet there is not much evidence that there is any causal connection between penalizing piracy and disposing people toward attempting to earn money by writing. Even Samuel Makore, the current executive director of ZIMCOPY, acknowledges that the organization has not identified any reliable means of measuring its success. He notes that it has mattered mainly as a managerial operation, which is not a small victory in the current policy-making climate: "it brought civil society together." This seems to mean that people from various sectors named in the original grant application—publishing, universities, law—met and agreed that copyright enforcement was a good thing. It is "complicated to show," the UNESCO report on

ZIMCOPY notes, that it succeeded in "creating more writers," but nevertheless local networks were built or reinforced. Capacity was built and an important affective identification was developed with the ideal of culture as a contributor to the future growth of Zimbabwe's economy.[16]

As it happens, Green Kephas Chilongo, the manager of ZIMCOPY when it received the IFCD grant, had previously been the head of a project to measure the economic contribution of Zimbabwe's creative and cultural industries (CCIs), which was awarded a US$99,000 IFCD grant. The goal of that project, which asked whether Zimbabwe's "vibrant culture and arts scene" could "contribute to its national economy and help the country escape poverty," was to encourage growth through measurement and promotion.[17] The announcement of the grant mentions data collection, data processing and analysis, and communicating the results to the public. This is classic cultural policy logic, wherein by "empirically demonstrating" the importance of CCIs to the national economy, the project will actually "contribute to their growth." By supporting and valuing culture's economic protagonism, you help to make it real. The same seems to be the case for penalizing piracy: there is not much data proving that piracy really threatens legitimate industry, but the idea that it does brings together interested groups in the cultural community. Investment in the ideal of penalizing piracy facilitates networking, which in turn facilitates project development, the writing of grant applications, festival planning, and so on. There is some boosting effect, even if it is not directly "delivered" by the original goals set out by the project.

* * *

The contrast with the approach to copyright that emerged in the more immediate postcolonial period is revealing. UNESCO is now regularly concerned with enforcing intellectual property regimes and copyright. What was once World Book Day is now World Book and Copyright Day. Yet in the 1960s, UNESCO had supported meetings at which the new postcolonial member nations sought to negotiate more lenient copyright terms, or even free use of works that were protected by copyrights in Europe and North America, in order to help establish their own publishing industries. Part of what they wanted was to be able to print books by famous international authors and sell them relatively inexpensively, much like the United States had done when it built its own robust industry by pirating books by British writers and selling them in inexpensive editions.

As chapter 4 detailed, the growth of the industry in postcolonial nations was stifled by the wealth and power of the existing Western firms. The postcolonial nations wanted to intervene in international legal arrangements such that the balance of wealth and power might shift more in their favor. Wirtén's work on the postcolonial copyright reform meetings, which were organized under UNESCO's auspices, emphasizes the impetus against "the chauvinistic so-called colonial clause" that had extended the Berne international copyright convention to "incorporating dominions and colonies of the original European signatories by proxy."[18] The new sovereign nations were each meant, upon independence, to agree to continue to adhere to the convention as it stood. Yet its terms made no sense for regions with fledging book industries that could not sell sufficient copies to expand their operations, could not offer attractive contracts to prospective local writers, did not have a network of public libraries or schools on which to rely for base sales, could not undersell US or Soviet donor propagandists who provided free or very inexpensive books, and could not convince many people who did want to read that things like attractive covers, sturdy bindings, smooth paper, and uniform type mattered.

Many of these nations therefore sought to negotiate something better than the Berne Convention, something that would reflect their unique situation. This led to the first African Study Meeting on Copyright in Brazzaville in 1963, which was jointly organized by the United International Bureaux for the Protection of Intellectual Property (BIRPI) and UNESCO. The Brazzaville meeting was followed by the Stockholm Conference in 1967, which resulted in a key document, the Protocol Regarding Developing Countries. In discussions of the protocol, which never significantly altered the terms of international copyright, the new postcolonial publishers asked, among other things, to be allowed to publish translations of works without substantial licensing fees. They also asked to modify the standard copyright term (at that time in force for 50 years after the author's death) in order to be able to cheaply reproduce works of special momentary political significance and to be able to freely use works for teaching and research purposes. They positioned their interventions within what Wirtén calls "a familiar triangle of aid, hunger, and food"—"book hunger," again. Europeans and North Americans were glutted with books (2000 pages per year!), whereas in India, a UNESCO delegate to the Stockholm conference noted, the average was 23 pages per person per year.[19] This idea of a hunger for physical material books reflected the consequential truth of an imbalance in the flow of paper-based cultural goods, learning materials, "knowledge" itself, from the developed to the developing world. It was also a story that served the interests of postcolonial publishers, who wanted lenient copyright terms so that their own young companies could thrive. The industry's interests and the idealization of the virtue of reading were tied up together.

At the time, the terms of the international legal copyright regime were being contested in the name of the development of local industries. Now, though, that regime is upheld and revered with largely the same ends in view. For agencies like ZIMCOPY, attacking piracy is virtuous because it is upholding the law and helping to build legal industries. The contrast is simple: there is a legitimate industry participating in national growth and protected by laws, and there are criminal forces ignoring the national interest and thwarting the legitimate legal regime to enrich themselves. For its part, UNESCO is positioned only to fund mechanisms to help encourage the enforcement of copyright. Those mechanisms need not even be evidentially successful in supporting the emergence of local writers or the expansion of the industry in general. Instead, the simple activity of enforcing copyright can be sold, to those who continue to provide UNESCO's base budget, as an effort to reward private enterprises and local initiatives that are producing vibrant creative economies. As an intervention into the sphere of book production, it is telling. In the activities currently under UNESCO's guidance it is no longer possible even to catch a glimpse of interest in the overarching structural problems that produced the so-called "book hunger." Instead, we are presented with the simple scenario of a local industry and legitimate entrepreneurial writers being undermined by criminal piracy. The fact that those pirates might be the only people providing readers with access to materials at feasible prices in places where they already shop is beside the point.

* * *

It is amusing and perhaps strange that one of the works celebrated in UNESCO's coverage of ZIMCOPY is NoViolet Bulawayo's 2013 *We Need New Names*—strange because the novel is so sympathetic to those struggling to survive on the outskirts of formal regulated economies. It follows a gang of children in Zimbabwe whose families were left with nothing after their homes and possessions were taken from them and they were resettled in a shantytown called Paradise. They are victims of Robert Mugabe's Operation Murambatsvina, or "Move the Trash," officially known also as Operation Restore Order. A government campaign beginning in 2005 to clear slums across the country, it caused the loss of homes and livelihoods for at least seven hundred thousand people. Mugabe and other officials characterized the operation as a crackdown on illegal housing and black-market activities and as an effort to reduce the spread of infectious disease in poor areas. Others, including the United Nations, describe it as a campaign to make large sections of the urban and rural poor, who form much of the internal opposition to Mugabe's government, homeless.

James Arnett has studied Bulawayo's interest in the humanitarian response to this catastrophe and in the broader situation of economic disarray in sub-Saharan Africa. With the global economic downturn, diminishing investments in development projects by foreign states, the rise of predatory loans offered on draconian terms, exceptionally high unemployment, and catastrophic levels of inflation, a nation like Zimbabwe is rarely considered for any sort of capital investment—and when it is, the work on offer is exceptionally temporary and badly paid. There is little manufacturing infrastructure and little consolidated large-scale agriculture. There are massive rural and urban poor populations living on very little. In *We Need New Names*, there is no work for the main character's parents near Paradise. Instead, Darling's mother trades at the border, and her father only comes home from itinerant work to die of AIDS in front of his daughter. What is left, in this context, for Darling and her friends, other than accepting charity? Hence the novel's emphasis on the mediation of suffering.[20]

Suffering on camera is one of the only means by which Zimbabwean children can have their needs met. To provide for themselves, they must display their suffering bodies and trade on their capacity for generating feelings in developed-world consumers. Nothing is expected of them except that they suffer in a telegenic way, decorously and not too aggressively—no shouting, no scary overeagerness to receive recompense.

The novel's wealthier characters sport "Save Darfur" and "Invisible Children" T-shirts, while charities and NGOs fight for people's attention and spare income. The book often depicts forms of slacktivism: virtual indulgence in feelings or postures of outrage and anger that betray little understanding of the true extent of the problem, the real causes of poverty, and so on. In Bulawayo's depiction, charities have nothing to do with helping people understand the circumstances that produce the conditions or how to mitigate them. They just manufacture images of suffering to secure charitable contributions. In a competitive marketplace, they need to sell the idea of donating to charity to those wealthy enough to give, so people in charity-logo T-shirts take pictures of suffering children to share on Instagram.

Bulawayo features centrally in Ikhide Ikheloa's controversial think piece "How Not to Write About Africa," which concludes, based on a review of the entries for the 2011 Caine Prize competition, that new writers view Africa "through a very narrow prism, all in a bid to win the Caine Prize." Ikheloa predicts Bulawayo's win for her story "Hitting Budapest," which became the first chapter in *We Need New Names*: "She sure can write, unfortunately her muse insists on sniffing around Africa's sewers."[21] This assessment draws from a familiar argument about how African literature circulates in Western markets. Critics have argued that writers pander to Western readers drawn to stories of "poverty porn" about "darkest Africa"; they produce extroverted or "self-anthropologizing" works that assume a non-African readership.[22] But, as Arnett points out, *We Need New Names* is actually less an instance of poverty porn than it is about the conditions of poverty porn's production. It takes as one of its core assumptions the prurient and in this case also humanitarian or activist gaze of the reader-consumer from the developed world. Through Darling, we see what it is to be looked upon and gawked at in sympathy, prurient fascination, scorn, outrage, and more, and we notice how her situation mirrors that of the Zimbabwean author interested in making a living by writing.

It is useful to compare *We Need New Names* with a novel by another celebrated Zimbabwean writer engaged with an earlier period in Zimbabwe's history: *Nervous Conditions*, by Tsitsi Dangarembga, published in 1988. *Nervous Conditions* is written from the point of view of an adult looking back at her childhood experience in a colonial education system that selected particular black children for education, the idea being that their families would somehow share in their success and select children would become leaders. The children are meant to be grateful for the largess of the white settlers. And Tambu is. But only at first.

Rhodesia was set up as a colony in the late nineteenth century by the British South Africa Company, which sought to extract the area's mineral wealth. The company had monopolistic trade rights in the region, command over the country's natural resources, and extraordinary powers of policing so long as it helped to ensure the "civilizing" and development of the natives. Its head was Cecil Rhodes, that exemplar of imperialist ideology and racism. The country having been colonized, resources in the process of being extracted, and people conscripted into horrible work for little or no pay, were they then supposed to be glad if a few were selected to receive a good Christian education? This is the brutal logic that *Nervous Conditions* depicts so well. It is exceedingly hard for Tambu to depart from the path laid out for her. She can't help believing in it, at least a little bit, because she does not want to be trapped her whole life, like her mother, in service to a man in a Shona village. Indeed, throughout the novel, the ideology of development appears to be a way of accommodating children and their families to a system of Pied-Piper-like extraction of "gifted" individuals from their communities, placing them into what seems to Tambu a reified world of higher-order, spiritualized pleasures—a "sublimation," she calls it, "with me as the sublimate."[23] Things in her rich uncle's Christian community are beautiful for no reason! Tambu finds this mind-blowing and seductive.

In one of the novel's early scenes, Tambu goes to the market to sell mealies that she farmed herself, in order to earn the money to pay school fees that her father will not provide. She does not manage to sell much, but she sees white people for the first time—their scent and thin papery skin horrify her—and the man who agreed to drive her to the market gets involved in a confrontation with a racist couple. Apparently oblivious to the limitations placed on a rural African child's schooling, they accuse her chaperone of exploiting her as child labor and insist that Tambu should be in school. Her chaperone eventually calms them down by telling a sad story which we, like Tambu, do not hear, because it is in English. Whatever the story is, it works: they give the man an amount of money that the mealies themselves would never have fetched. Tambu's work is not rewarded; instead, she becomes the object of charity because she has a sad story. This upsets her, but at least she can pay her school fees.[24]

Contrast this with the most notable market scene in *We Need New Names*. The day that "NGO" arrives, the children run to meet the truck. They know not to crowd the NGO workers; they know not to yell too loudly. They know they will need to pose for photos. A local woman, Sis Betty, acts as intermediary. She counsels everyone on the proper decorum: smile, say thank you, look pleased but not too pleased. Don't be demanding, don't clamor. Darling notices that the photographer is especially interested in photos of her very young pregnant friend and of Godknows, a boy whose shorts are torn at the back, exposing his rear end. She describes his photography as "taking away again" and wonders who will see the images. She notices, also, the "shiny things" on the fingers of one of the NGO staff. They are glinting in the sun.[25]

Both novels revile the idea of the benevolence of the white savior. In *Nervous Conditions*, the white settlers' charity, with the attendant implication that the colonial order is itself a gift to the colonized, is belied by the broad fact, emphasized throughout the novel, that their status is premised on the dispossession of those who are then supposed to be grateful for their (subsequent, belated) largess. In *We Need New Names*, the idea of the "gift" given by NGO is undermined because Darling experiences the photography as a kind of capture. The fact of the children's dependence on the arrival of this truck is treated as a product of the history of uneven colonial and neocolonial economies of which NGO workers have been beneficiaries. What could the woman's flashing ring refer to but Cecil Rhodes's murderous, profitable diamond mines?

The contrasts between the novels are also striking, though. The market scene in *Nervous Conditions* is part of a journey of development. Tambu learns that she does not want to be subject to charity. She wants to be educated and earn a living for herself by other means. *Nervous Conditions* presents the power to write one's story as the fruit of the narrator's postcolonial developmental journey. Having experienced development, Tambu is ready, by the end of her story, to assess it and to fault it where necessary, and her work will enter the market as an intervention into an otherwise unquestioned tale of progress. It is largely about gaining a voice; about being critical. In *We Need New Names*, the circumscribed subjects of charity have little scope to aspire to anything better. They fixate instead on fantasies of exit. Bulawayo's work thus presents the sad story—the poverty porn—as one that fails to offer a conduit to anything. It is, instead, quite simply exhausting. The storytelling that one is positioned to do is less a matter of gaining a voice than of having to accept posturing as a victim. The novel is again, in this respect, a self-reflexive work about not wanting to be pigeonholed. It resents the uneven relations that characterize the literary field, which ensure the extroverted reliance of the African literary sphere on foundation-backed donor support and American consumers.

Pushing the comparison further, *Nervous Conditions* is ultimately a work that longs for inclusion and that laments the exclusions dictated by racist colonial hegemonies. The political horizon of the novel is, basically, more autonomously determined inclusion and more effective economic protagonism. *We Need New Names*, in contrast, is a novel about, and of course created by, the demise of fantasies of full employment. It is a novel befitting the end of faith in incorporative or "absorptive" economies.[26] It is about superfluity and the rise of the NGO, literary and otherwise, and about a diminishment of options for the African writer who hopes to secure some part of a dwindling audience for literary expression. Its political horizon is harder to discern, but it is something like the end of the humanitarian-industrial complex—of the spectacularized suffering of the impoverished African child, the slacktivist T-shirt, the voluntourism, the conditions of economic destitution and the suffering-child-as-spectacle that those conditions help to advance.

Recall that the Caine Prize, which Bulawayo herself won, and which has been one of the most important supports for the development of African writers in recent years, is funded by the Oppenheimer Memorial Trust, which was founded with Ernest Oppenheimer's money, much of which came from gold and diamond mining. That glinting jeweled ring again—the exploited workers, profits accumulating in the coffers of the European parent firms, and so on. Bulawayo has the NGO worker sport her fancy ring in a shantytown in Zimbabwe because she wants us to remember that humanitarian aid is a product of, rather than a solution to, a larger set of uneven relations. Those relations are there in the NGO's photographs. They are also there in the Caine Prize, in the donor-backed African literary field, which is characterized by a widening gulf between wealth and deprivation—a gulf shared throughout the global English-language literary milieu in our era of decline.

Bulawayo's novel thus glimpses, with remarkable clarity, what necessarily delimits the success of a project like ZIMCOPY. The development of an industry that requires leisured consumers with nontrivial disposable income depends on a regime of relatively full employment and the kind of attendant "healthy" tax base that supports the social policies that enable the emergence of a sizeable reading culture. Elite forms of literary expression depend heavily upon this regime. It seems unlikely to be restored, or at least not in its old postwar form.

Nor is Bulawayo at all unkind to pirates! Some of the most exuberant and skewering writing in the novel is in sympathy with the band of children who wander hungry through the wealthy neighborhoods that border their own, gorging themselves on fruit stolen from the fenced-in trees.

Conclusion

THIS STUDY OF UNESCO'S HISTORY of literary programming reveals the fundamental structuring connections among the production of the world-literary milieu, liberal cultural policy making, and underlying economic conditions.

The first era of UNESCO's interest in books and literature reflected anxiety over the anticipated collapse of Europe's formal empires. The Collection of Representative Works supported the superior role taken by experts from the developed nations in directing the course of world history in the aftermath of empire. In this respect, it accorded with the establishment of a cosmopolitan liberalism whose key broker was the development-oriented US foreign policy establishment, which promoted its international operations and entailments as the building of partnerships in the making of a new global community—a community with US-style social organization at its "vital center." In its early years, initial visionary plans aside, the Collection of Representative Works was in practice predominantly a means of garnering support for the translation of classic works of world literature into English and French. It backed the authority and flourishing of those languages as the media through which a substantial global cultural storehouse would be constructed. This was justified by the idea that evolution toward perfected humanity would require recourse to and reverence for the unity amid diversity that this storehouse would naturally contain. A fantasized sympathetic global community, committed to enlightened liberal democratic capitalism, would cohere around such reverence, backed by an endlessly dynamic and expanding economy made up of partner nations sharing in a generalized wealth, with standards of living improving indefinitely.

This postwar "boom" period of faith in infinite, unconstrained economic growth, and the funding of social programs and cultural infrastructure that emerged with it, were inseparable from a resource-extracting and intensively accumulative drive whose massive profits were of course never to be practicably globalized. The middle period of the 1970s involved a rejection, crystallized in the cultural policy debates and the failed struggles for a New World Information and Communication Order, of much of what the Collective of Representative Works represented. Whereas UNESCO's early history is evidence of general support in the global policy field for the ongoing imperial trusteeship of the white nations and developed economies, this support was eventually displaced by reformist attempts—including significantly anti-imperialist, anti-racist, and anti-capitalist efforts—to establish some sort of genuinely balanced or "humanized" system of cultural production and exchange.

In the 1970s, UNESCO partook of a vibrant movement of protest, a thriving international resistance to the cultural and economic values of the liberal capitalist developed world, and an insistence that white universalism and developmentalism were neocolonial impositions that prevented the postcolonial nations from achieving fair integration into the global capitalist markets for labor and goods. In debating the merits of instituting a New International Economic Order, some developing nations argued for an increase in development assistance with no strings attached, or for improvements in the terms of trade that would ensure the equitable pricing of raw materials and the reduction or elimination of tariffs. Their Charter of Economic Rights and Duties of States, which was only ever partially and temporarily implemented, said that members should have the right to "regulate and exercise authority over foreign investment" and even to "nationalize, expropriate or transfer ownership of foreign property."[1] We can understand this, as Konstantina Tzouvala does, as the inevitable outcome of the global spread of the ideology of capitalist modernization, backed by the constitutive bureaucratic nationalism of the United Nations. Or we can read it, in Aijaz Ahmad's less damning terms, as a unique balance of forces that arose from the revolutionary upheavals and radical nationalisms of the 1960s—a balance of forces that resulted in the explicit endorsement by the United Nations of the "fundamental aspirations of Third World economic nationalism."[2] Neither quite accounts for the way in which the developing nations took advantage of the fissures produced by destabilizing economic crises.

The New World Information and Communication Order was the UNESCO parallel to the New International Economic Order. It aimed to right imbalances in the distribution of news, information, and culture through, for example, technology transfers from the developed to the developing nations, targeted at expanding industry infrastructure and training professional personnel. The fact that it was made to fail is telling. What arose thereafter, becoming dominant by the mid-1980s, is something more like a neoliberal de-commodification. In this formation there no longer seems to be any tension between asserting the "inherent" and "immeasurable" humanizing value of culture and trumpeting its increasing role in grounding economic development. Economic development is itself positioned as the ultimate humanism. Developing economically dynamic cultural industries becomes the organization's core work. Much of this activity is still explicitly opposed to neocolonial developmentalism—the kind that is too insensitive to local conditions, too obsessed with rapid growth, and too hierarchical. The activity is driven, instead, by what John Pat Leary has described as "humanitarian innovation's anti-bureaucratic ethos of autonomy and creativity." This replaces the language of development with the idealization of creative empowerment, grounded in innate or premodern capacities for resilience and autonomous community.[3]

UNESCO's history of cultural policy making has consistently responded to pressure to address the realities of wealth and deprivation, in the cultural sphere but also more broadly: from its moment of support for the postwar development establishment's emphasis on raising "living standards"; through the era of lament over cultural imperialism, systemic underdevelopment, and the necessary recourse to culture as "humanizing," de-commodified care; to the contemporary investment in the value of culture as management of unease and a conduit to ongoing economic dynamism.

The trajectory of UNESCO's literary programming runs in parallel: from the postwar period of serious investment in the literary as a site of global communication, interconnectivity, and sympathetic community; through the period of worry over underdeveloped access to books and the skills needed to appreciate them effectively; to the contemporary period of creative-cities networking and city-branding through the trumpeting of a vibrant literary culture and tradition. Overall, policy makers' investment in the idealization of the literary as a humanizing global force in world affairs seems to have declined, and the development of underdeveloped literary industries is no longer much of a focus. The association of literature with left-liberal de-commodification lives on, but mainly as a means of helping to brand a marketable heritage in festival sites and tourist experiences aimed at a relatively wealthy elite.

* * *

Individual literary works have served a wide variety of purposes throughout this history. Their tendencies cannot be reduced to a single model. I have highlighted, instead, some representative instances, in which the text in question is fundamentally linked to the policy making situation, which is for its own part inseparable from broader political-economic currents. UNESCO supported the publication and circulation in English translation of *Snow Country*, which helped to secure Kawabata's global reputation as a spokesperson for PEN-style literary internationalism, committed to the artist's complete freedom from any sort of political bullying or necessary responsibility. As a novel that codifies and romanticizes Japanese folk traditions, from geisha to Chijimi clothmaking, it both accords with and supports UNESCO's activities then and now.

The realities addressed by UNESCO in the era of the real flourishing of cultural policy as a site of political possibility feature quite differently, in turn, in "The Doum Tree of Wad Hamid." The policy-making mindset and the set of worries arising during that period help to explain the nature of Salih's fascination with the incorporation of the precapitalist village of Wad Hamid into the postcolonial nation via the museumization of the doum tree. The story is largely about the correct affective disposition for the policy maker: ambivalent about modernization, sad about what is lost, eager to preserve what can be saved, but reconciled to the inevitability of development. The same is true of *The Heart of Redness*, although there, as befits UNESCO's more recent history, the novel provides a fantasy of a locally directed and mutually beneficial form of economic integration that can solve persistent problems of underdevelopment and underemployment. There is no question in the novel about the value of integration into market-based commercial culture, and no real worry about anything being lost. It is ultimately comic and exuberant rather than mournful. Culture-based tourism, secured by heritage status, is celebrated as a species of local community-owned industry that can strategically commercialize culture without threatening anything of authentic value. Economic development is itself presented as an agent of heritage preservation.

Finally, in *We Need New Names*, the general phenomenon of imbalance in the infrastructure of global communications, which is of such concern for UNESCO, is a conditioning reality in the world of the novel. But where UNESCO now participates in demonizing piracy, Bulawayo's work suggests why, in conditions of worsening underdevelopment, the ideal of some fuller expansion of the legitimate publishing industry might be a pipe dream. The ideal of full workforce participation is itself presented as residual, outmoded, unrealistic. The work that is available is exploitative, badly paid, dangerous, and beneath human dignity. And the informal alternatives to work, such as becoming dependent objects of humanitarian charity, are no better. The novel implicitly impugns the uneven relations of the literary world. It links the literary reader to the wealthy dispenser of charity, eager to consume images of suffering others. It is thus a perfect document for an era in which the aspiration to be literary, like the aspiration to full employment—fully regulated, fully taxed— seems increasingly fantastical.

* * *

It is hard to be conclusive about UNESCO's future. It does seem, though, that the United States is not destined to play much of a role in it. After Palestine was recognized as a member in 2011—and its status as a legitimate state thus implicitly granted—the United States stopped making its regular contribution of more than $80 million per year, which was at the time about 22 percent of the organization's budget. It lost its vote in the General Conference, which is the main policy-making engine, but retained a say in some areas of activity, including the selection of a new director general. But in 2017, in its general drift toward unilateralism and supported by an apparently rising animus against social spending on arts and culture, the United States announced a more complete withdrawal from UNESCO, diminishing its role even further to that of an observer state.

China has meanwhile increased its involvement, lately presenting itself as the benevolent and responsible alternative to a flagrantly selfish US administration. It seems to back cultural programs to the extent that they help to establish its influence in economic and political affairs and to secure its ability to present itself as a benevolent force and leader, able to aggregate, direct, and when necessary control competing global players. It has announced generous financial contributions to UNESCO programs, extending to tens of millions in extrabudgetary funds, while also seeking a leadership role within the organization, as it has done at other international governance bodies, including the International Telecommunications Union and the United Nations' Department of Economic and Social Affairs.[4] A recent *Foreign Policy* article on China's bid for power within UNESCO states that "China is simply using its growing economic and political clout at the U.N. to pick up distressed assets abandoned by the US and its allies and repurpose them to serve its strategic goals."[5] These goals include advocating tighter Internet regulations and, perhaps, attempting to encourage a generally more permissive attitude toward state censorship and repression.

When the Chinese president, Xi Jinping, spoke to UNESCO in 2014, his interpretation of the organization's founding commitments was deeply politically invested. Harmony amidst diversity and unity without uniformity are reframed in his speech as coinciding with his "keenly-felt conviction that an attitude of equality and modesty is required if one wants to truly understand the various civilizations." The alternative, of too brashly asserting one's own perspective, is described as "a condescending attitude," which may "risk antagonizing" the civilization in question. "The ocean is vast for it refuses no rivers," he stated. We must thus work hard to avoid suggesting that civilizations should "copy" one another, "mechanically or blindly." That would be "like cutting one's toes just to fit his shoes." The only way to avoid the "clash of civilizations" is by insisting on this "inclusiveness" and on mutual respect for and within cultural differences. "This is like what we Chinese often say, 'Radish or cabbage, each to his own delight,'" he explained.[6] He neatly impugned faulting a nation for its practices or implying that there is one right way to do things. The implication is that even UNESCO-backed frameworks and guidelines, which, after all, have no legal force, should make clear that there is no toe-cutting implied, nothing forced upon any government, nothing that takes precedence over the inherent value of civilizations' differences.

Xi interspersed these statements about his own take on UNESCO's founding rationale, backed by choice pieces of Chinese folk wisdom, with snippets of China's great civilizational history and contribution to human progress and an affirmation of the Chinese government's commitment to scientific and technological development and the "continued process of exploiting nature." It is in this context that he mentioned Chinese benevolence within UNESCO, referring especially to Africa—as a continent with numerous dramatically poor economies, but also as an area of the world that has been for decades, and increasingly now, of acute strategic interest to the Chinese government and Chinese corporations. He listed, in particular, the expansion of the Great Wall Fellowship program, which funds 75 international students to attend Chinese universities each year (and reserves some of those spots for African students), and the Chinese-funded Funds-in-Trust program, which uses information and communications technologies to expand capacity at teacher-training facilities in Africa.[7]

Xi's emphasis on Chinese funds allocated especially to Africa speaks to decades of growing levels of Chinese foreign aid, as well as Chinese state-backed and corporate loans and investments, targeting so-called "emerging market economies" in Africa. Most African nations have debts to China, and China's own new development bank, the Asian Infrastructure Investment Bank (AIIB), which since its founding in 2015 has entered into more than twenty-five development agreements to fund projects worth some $4 billion, has identified Africa as its next area for expansion.[8] The United States has not joined the AIIB, but Britain and other European countries have, eager to participate in its lending projects and to secure an advantage for their own companies in competition with American and Japanese firms that are developing projects in emerging markets. This, combined with the fact that the International Monetary Fund "now includes the Yuan as a global reserve-trading currency, alongside the dollar, pound, and euro," leads some observers to conclude that China is effectively establishing "alternative institutions" that "break the hegemonic control of global economic institutions by the USA."[9] In this context, Africa has become a testing ground for China's economic and political ambitions.

The Chinese interest in UNESCO appears to be one "soft power" manifestation of this broader activity. China is designing and backing UNESCO programs especially focused on the regions of the world where it is currently most involved in commodities manufacturing, resource extraction, land grabs for crops such as rubber, and commercial food production—there are many Chinese mining companies, agribusinesses, consumer goods manufacturers, tourism outfits, and so on in Africa—and it is doing this as an accompaniment to the global expansion of its power. According to one source, there were just over 227,000 Chinese workers in Africa at the end of 2016. That same year, the gross revenues of Chinese companies' construction projects in Africa was $50 billion. Chinese foreign aid has increased at a rate of 14 percent per year since 2003 and has tended to be targeted specifically at what will advance a corporate developmentalist agenda: technical assistance in industrial development and in transitioning from agrarian cultivation to commercial agriculture, training in science and technology, and programs facilitating access to information and communications technology.[10]

This investment is not quite a sign of China's permanent economic security. China's lending and development regime is built on a massive, decades-long proletarianization of the Chinese population, which has tended to force their abandonment of rural enclaves, migration into cities, and entry into poorly paid work. The profits from international lending now uniquely equip China to assuage the unrest that results when those cities are themselves abandoned, workers are made superfluous, and they can no longer depend on escape to their villages as refuge. The Chinese government can afford economic stimuli, job creation via public works, and some concessions to workers' demands in part because of its international lending and development activities as an "integral market for the debt of deficit-dependent countries elsewhere."[11] In other words, development in Africa is part of what makes it possible for China to offset some of the social fallout from the way in which, in fact, "the Chinese economy as a whole appears to follow the same pattern of deindustrialization and informalization seen worldwide."[12] Expansion into Africa has been a means of securing creditor status and a classic spatial fix providing access to land, raw material, markets, and labor.

The incorporation of China into capitalist social relations continues, then, but not, crucially, into the kind of workforce that characterized the United States in the 1950s or Britain in the 1890s, as, notoriously by now, fewer workers are needed to achieve higher rates of productive efficiency. In the words of the Chuang collective, whose work is focused on capitalism in China, as "the percentage of the population required to produce a given quantity of goods and extract a given quantity of natural resources diminishes over time," then "it becomes difficult to reproduce proletarians *as productive workers*."[13] Land is developed, resources extracted, but workers are only fitfully and partially exploited in temporary arrangements and short-term projects that fail to provide them with much material benefit, motivation, or futurity. Chuang writes that the "traditional characteristics associated with the surplus population (informality, precarity, illegality) have again become relatively 'normal' characteristics of the laboring population as a whole."[14] In other words, development without development. Modernization without modernity.

In *We Need New Names*, the only paid labor observed locally is working for Chinese contractors who are quickly building a luxury shopping mall. The management is Chinese, the manual labor is African. We gather that the pay is low enough, and the work so temporary, that even people who could secure this work can't see the point. When Darling and her friends visit the mall, a site manager boasts: "We build you big mall. All nice shops inside, Gucci, Louis Vuitton, Versace, and so on so on."[15] In a country that lacks anything like adequate employment for most people, a shopping mall is clearly a niche affair. We are asked to weigh the posh brand names against the threadbare tattered behind of Godknows's pants, much photographed by the NGO workers in the humanitarian truck scene that follows soon after.

In China itself, as elsewhere, the cultural economy is a branch of the service sector that is available to absorb some of the people who cannot be incorporated into the productive workforce. The rate of absorption depends on region and socioeconomic status. In the wealthier global cities, such as Shanghai and Beijing, which boast some of the most lavish creative neighborhoods and respected creative-economy boosters (the M50 Art District, the 798 Art Zone), there are high-paying jobs in the creative, heritage, and tourism sectors. They hardly need direct funding from UNESCO programming, but many have UNESCO branding attached. There are also cultural workers in what the Chuang collective describes as the "vast state-funded, semi-speculative complexes of welfare and middle-income service work, most visible in the education, healthcare and 'non-profit' industries."[16] And then there is the expanding dispossessed periphery, often the target of nonprofit work and welfare provision—including, in the emerging markets, UNESCO's own programs, backed by Chinese and other funding, that encourage the development of educated and skilled labor.

It is impossible to say exactly how UNESCO cultural policy will change under the dominance of Chinese interests, or indeed how permanent that dominance will be. UNESCO itself may not survive much longer. What seems likely, though, given the history we do know, is that the organization will continue along the path it has taken in recent years. It will, for now, go on supporting "guideline" policy making to back the development of cultural heritage and tourism resources for creative-economy development in the centers of wealth, while attempting to make people productive and employable, or at least more resilient, at the expanding peripheries.

Notes

Introduction

1. I draw largely from accounts of economic downturn by Robert Brenner and the Endnotes research collective, while I also emphasize, following Claus Offe and Giovanni Arrighi, the crises in state legitimacy and threats to US hegemony that attend this downturn. Brenner pinpoints a boom period of prosperity lasting roughly from the 1940s through the late 1960s, a general downturn beginning in the mid-1960s, and then "slowed growth and increasing economic turbulence from 1973," with "reduced economic dynamism and declining economic performance" (*The Economics of Global Turbulence*, xix). Endnotes describes how low demand for labor has led to a worldwide decline in labor's share of income. In attempting to manage this, the state "has taken on massive amounts of debt, and has periodically been forced to undertake 'reforms'"—the reforms often associated with neoliberal governance, under which we witness a "falling away of social protections" that ultimately serves to deepen and spread uncertainty yet further ("A History of Separation," 76).

2. Warwick Research Collective, *Combined and Uneven Development*, 19.

3. Cheah, *What Is a World?*, 2, 16. Subsequent references appear in the body of the text.

4. Warwick Research Collective, "WReC's Reply," 544.

5. For a longer treatment of WReC's approach, see Brouillette and Thomas, "Forum: *Combined and Uneven Development*," 509–16.

6. Macherey and Balibar, "Literature as an Ideological Form: Some Marxist Propositions," 4–12.

7. Emre, *Paraliterary*; see also Barnhisel, *Cold War Modernists*; Bennett, *Workshops of Empire*; Saunders, *Who Paid the Piper?*

8. Schryer, *Maximum Feasible Participation*; Ferguson, *Top Down*.

9. Lewis and Miller, "Introduction," 1–2.

10. Huxley, "Colonies and Freedom," 106.

11. Hewison, *Culture and Consensus*, 45.

12. Litt, *The Muses, the Masses, and the Massey Commission*.

13. Tzouvala, "Letters of Blood and Fire," 113; Rist, *The History of Development*, 79–88.

14. Arrighi, *The Long Twentieth Century*, 69. To be clear, Arrighi's argument is ultimately that the United States struggles to maintain its hold over these instruments, as its hegemony is threatened and then set on a course toward "terminal crisis."

15. Fraser, "Expropriation and Exploitation in Racialized Capitalism," 175.

16. See Apter, *The Pan-African Nation*.

17. For an account of social regulation and economic development, see De Angelis, "Neoliberal Governance."

18. Franssen and Kuipers, "Sociology of Literature and Publishing in the Early 21st Century," 291.

Chapter 1

1. UNESCO, "Report of UNESCO," 3.

2. Ibid., 8.

3. Ibid., 3.

4. United Nations General Assembly, "Declaration on the Establishment," 96.

5. United Nations Economic and Social Council, "Resolutions Adopted," 44.

6. UNESCO, "Report of UNESCO," 4.

7. Ibid., 5–6.

8. Ibid., 8.

9. Ibid., 10–11.

10. Ibid., 12–15.

11. Besterman, *Unesco: Peace in the Minds of Men*, 64.

12. Mileva, "UNESCO and World Literary Values," 98.

13. Ibid., 98–99.

14. UNESCO, *UNESCO Collection*, 15.

15. Huxley, *UNESCO: Its Purpose and Philosophy*.

16. UNESCO, "Constitution."

17. Rist, *The History of Development*, 70–72; Mazower, *Governing the World*, 273–78.

18. Truman, "Inaugural Address."

19. Huxley, *UNESCO: Its Purpose and Philosophy*, 53.

20. Ibid., 53–54.

21. Ibid., 50.

22. Huxley and Deane, *The Future of the Colonies*, 8.

23. Ibid.

24. Huxley, "Colonies and Freedom," 106.

25. Sluga, "UNESCO," 406.

26. Sewell, *UNESCO and World Politics*, 111.

27. Huxley, "Colonies and Freedom," 108.

28. Emphasis in original. Quoted in Dorn and Ghodsee, "The Cold War Politicization of Literacy," 377.

29. Huxley, "Colonies and Freedom," 108.

30. Huxley and Deane, *The Future of the Colonies*, 31.

31. Huxley, "Colonies and Freedom," 109.

32. Huxley and Deane, *The Future of the Colonies*, 8.

33. Quoted in Sluga, "UNESCO," 408.

34. Sluga, "UNESCO," 415.

35. Prashad, *The Darker Nations*, 284.

36. Hazzard, *Postwar Anti-Racism*, 35–62.

37. Smith, "Biology and Values," 234.

38. Ibid., 238.

39. Huxley, Haddon, and Carr-Saunders, *We Europeans*.

40. Brattain, "Race, Racism, and Antiracism," 1388.

41. Rangil, "The Politics of Neutrality," 40.

42. Sluga, "UNESCO," 395.

43. Ibid., 407.

Chapter 2

1. Walker, "Unbinding the Japanese Novel," 54.

2. Matsugu, "The War," 1.

3. Österling, "Award Ceremony Speech."

4. Bennett, *Workshops of Empire*.

5. Schwartz, *Creating Faulkner's Reputation*, 5.

6. Walker, "Unbinding the Japanese Novel," 120.

7. Brown, "Yasunari Kawabata," 375.

8. Schwartz, *Creating Faulkner's Reputation*, 4.

9. Schlesinger, *The Vital Center*, 248–49.

10. Ibid., 244.

11. Ibid., 245.

12. Doherty, "PEN International," 208.

13. Rosenstein, *Understanding Cultural Policy*, 19–24.

14. Laves, *UNESCO*, 3.

15. Ibid., 2

16. Ibid., 4–5.

17. Klein, *Cold War Orientalism*, 26.

18. Ibid., 13.

19. Walker, "Unbinding the Japanese Novel," 76.

20. Strauss, "Unusual Problems," cited in Walker, "Unbinding the Japanese Novel," 59.

21. Klein, *Cold War Orientalism*, 14.

22. Kawabata, *Snow Country*, vi. Subsequent page numbers appear in the body of the chapter.

23. Matsugu, "In the Service," 245–46.

24. Ibid., 245–46.

25. Matsugu, "The War," 172.

26. Matsugu, "In the Service," 248.

27. Brown, "Yasunari Kawabata," 378.

28. Ibid., 379.

29. Österling, "Award Ceremony Speech."

Chapter 3

1. UNESCO, *Cultural Policy*, 10.

2. Rosenstein, *Understanding Cultural Policy*, 54–55.

3. UNESCO, *Cultural Policy*, 10.

4. Emphasis added by Perry. Perry, "Immutable Mobiles," 178.

5. Quoted in ibid., 176.

6. Ibid., 180.

7. UNESCO, *Cultural Policy*, 11.

8. Ibid., 44.

9. UNESCO, *Intergovernmental Conference on Cultural Policies*, 7–8.

10. On the use of the National Endowment for the Arts in the effort to "manage social problems," see Yúdice, "The Privatization of Culture," which argues that government "sought to use subsidies for cultural activism as a way of channeling the expression of opposition"—one part of a broader set of activities of "crisis management" to handle the "deterioration of social control unleashed by migration to the cities and unemployment among blacks and other racial minorities" (21).

11. McCarthy, "Cold War to Cultural Development," 107.

12. Ibid., 108–9.

13. Becker, *Human Capital*, 2, 159. Quoted in Dorn and Ghodsee, "The Cold War Politicization of Literacy," 384.

14. Dorn and Ghodsee, "The Cold War Politicization of Literacy," 384.

15. Ibid., 390.

16. Ibid., 393.

17. Quoted in ibid., 393–94.

18. Ibid., 394.

19. Quoted in ibid., 390.

20. Ibid., 392.

21. UNESCO, *The Experimental World Literacy Programme and its Global Evaluation*, 8.

22. Ibid., 8.

23. UNESCO, *The Experimental World Literacy Programme: A Critical Assessment*, 121.

24. Ibid.

25. Ibid., 122.

26. UNESCO, *World Conference on Cultural Policies*, 178.

27. Ibid., 178–79.

28. Ibid., 179.

29. Ibid., 190.

30. Offe, *Contradictions of the Welfare State*, 149.

31. Salih, "The Doum Tree of Wad Hamid," 14. Subsequent page numbers appear in the body of the text.

32. Federici, *Caliban and the Witch*, 9.

33. Ibid.

Chapter 4

1. Behrstock, "UNESCO and the World of Books," 21.

2. UNESCO, "Charter of the Book."

3. Altbach's publishing record in this area is extensive. Relevant research includes "The Dilemma of Success: Universities in Advanced Developing Countries"; "Key Issues of Textbook Provision in the Third World"; "Servitude of the Mind? Education, Dependency and Neocolonialism"; "Third World Publishers and the International Knowledge System"; and "The University as Center and Periphery."

4. Darnton, "What Is the History of Books?" 67, 75.

5. Ibid., 67.

6. Ibid.

7. Ibid., 78.

8. Ibid., 76.

9. Ibid., 81.

10. On UNESCO's copyright reform advocacy, addressed further in chapter 6, see also Altbach, "Literary Colonialism," 226–36; Barker and Escarpit, "Copyright," 94–98; Ravelonanosy, "New Copyright Revision," 32; and Wirtén, *Cosmopolitan Copyright*, 49–67.

11. Darnton, "What Is the History of Books?" 65.

12. Slaughter, *Human Rights Inc.*, 281.

13. Gilman, *Mandarins of the Future*, 5.

14. Ibid., 5–6.

15. Arrighi, *Adam Smith in Beijing*, 256–57.

16. UNESCO, *Medium-Term Plan*, viii.

17. "Toward a New World Order," 4.

18. UNESCO, *Medium-Term Plan*, xxiii.

19. Ibid., xxiv–xxv.

20. Ibid., xxv, 11.

21. Ibid., xxix.

22. Ibid., xxiii, xxxi.

23. Ibid., 11. See also the United Nations General Assembly, "Declaration on the Establishment," which affirms "the right of all . . . under foreign occupation, alien and colonial domination or apartheid to restitution and full compensation for the exploitation and depletion of, and damages to, the natural resources and all other resources of those States, territories and peoples" (4ff).

24. UNESCO, *Medium-Term Plan*, 12.

25. Ibid., ix.

26. Ibid., 89.

27. See articles 58–59 in UNESCO, "Records of the General Conference, Paris 1964," 173.

28. Behrstock, "UNESCO and the World of Books," 22.

29. UNESCO, "Records of the General Conference, Paris 1964," 173.

30. Escarpit, *The Book Revolution*, 159.

31. Barker and Escarpit, *The Book Hunger*, 15.

32. Ibid., 16.

33. Ibid., 131.

34. Altbach, "Literary Colonialism," 234.

35. Altbach and Rathgeber, *Publishing in the Third World*, 8–9.

36. Smith, *The Impact of Transnational Book Publishing*, 10.

37. Ibid., 3, 8.

38. Kotei, *The Book Today*, 138.

39. Altbach and Rathgeber, *Publishing in the Third World*, 6.

40. Giffard, *UNESCO and the Media*, 20.

41. *Fourth Conference of Heads of State or Government*, 73.

42. Ibid., 88.

43. Schiller, "Decolonization of Information," 41.

44. Wells, *The UN, UNESCO*, 40.

45. For outlines of these goals, see UNESCO, *Anatomy of an International Year* and UNESCO, *Books for All: A Programme of Action*.

46. See the comments of Russian representative Sergei Losev recorded in UNESCO, *Many Voices, One World*, the report of the MacBride Commission established by UNESCO to study international communications issues (172, 279).

47. Finn, "How to Lose," 42.

48. Wells, *The UN, UNESCO*, 97.

49. UNESCO, "Declaration on Fundamental Principles," 103.

50. UNESCO, *Many Voices*, 6.

51. Ibid., 22.

52. Ibid., 37.

53. This argument is in Giffard, *UNESCO and the Media*, xix; and Wells, *The UN, UNESCO*, 113.

54. Barnett and Piggford, *Manual on Book and Library Activities*, 62, 60.

55. Richards, "The Soviet Overseas Information Empire," 210, 212.

56. Travis, "Middlebrow Culture," 469.

57. Benjamin, *U.S. Books Abroad*, 70.

58. Ibid., 70–72.

59. Tzouvala, "Letters of Blood and Fire," 143.

60. Wallerstein, "Modernization," 133.

61. Tzouvala, "Letters of Blood and Fire," 122.

62. United Nations, "Charter of the United Nations," article 55.

Chapter 5

1. McNally, "From Financial Crisis to World-Slump," 52.
2. Smith, "Imperialism in the Twenty-First Century," n.p.
3. Ibid.
4. Benanav and Clegg, "Misery and Debt," 585; Clover, *Riot. Strike. Riot,* 135.
5. For some indicative material not referenced here, see Mikić, *Measuring the Economic Contribution,* and UNCTAD, UNDP, UNESCO, WIPO, ITC, *Creative Economy Report.*
6. UNESCO, "Creative Cities Network."
7. Ibid.
8. "Krakow City of Literature," 6. Subsequent page numbers appear in the body of the chapter.
9. "Dublin UNESCO City of Literature," 99. Subsequent page numbers appear in the body of the chapter.
10. UNESCO, "Convention on the Protection and Promotion." All references in the following text are to this unpaginated document.
11. UNESCO, *International Fund for Cultural Diversity,* 28, 3.
12. Ibid., 3, 5.
13. Ibid., 8–9.
14. Ibid., 3.
15. Bokova, "The Power of Culture."
16. Mda, *The Heart of Redness,* 31. Subsequent references appear in the body of the text.
17. Mda, *When People Play People,* 55–56.
18. Ibid., 131.

Chapter 6

1. UNESCO, "Copyright: A Lifeline."
2. UNESCO, "Developing a National Strategy."
3. UNESCO, "Copyright: A Lifeline."
4. Ibid.
5. Bgoya and Jay, "Publishing in Africa," 4.
6. Wirtén, *Cosmopolitan Copyright,* 62.
7. Bgoya and Jay, "Publishing in Africa," 5.
8. Ibid., 6.
9. Ibid., 7.
10. Staunton, "Publishing for Pleasure," 50.
11. On literature as a nonprofit sector in Africa, see Strauhs, *African Literary NGOs.*
12. Staunton, "Publishing for Pleasure," 52.
13. Ibid.
14. See Harris, "Hot Reads."
15. Wirtén, *Cosmopolitan Copyright,* 49–50.

16. UNESCO, "Copyright: A Lifeline."

17. UNESCO, "Measuring the Economic Contribution of Cultural Industries."

18. Wirtén, *Cosmopolitan Copyright*, 50.

19. Ibid., 56.

20. Arnett, "Taking Pictures."

21. Ikheloa, "The 2011 Caine Prize."

22. See Ede, "Narrative Moment," and Julien, "The Extroverted African Novel."

23. Dangarembga, *Nervous Conditions*, 94.

24. Ibid., 28–30.

25. Bulawayo, *We Need New Names*, 53–59.

26. On the absorption and non-absorption of labor see Clover, "Fanon," which argues: "If the underdeveloped nations have become more developed [though they never had fully developed absorptive economies], creeping or lurching forward, the developed nations have become overdeveloped in ways that have effectively moved them not forward but back toward a political economy which is, if not properly colonial (whatever that might mean), non-absorptive *in a way that functionally replicates coloniality*. This is our present" (41, emphasis in the original).

Conclusion

1. See United Nations General Assembly, "Resolutions Adopted by the General Assembly," 3281 (XXIX).

2. Tzouvala, *Letters of Blood and Fire*; Ahmad, "Globalization and Culture," 100.

3. Leary, "Innovation and the Neoliberal Idioms of Development."

4. Lynch and Groll, "As U.S. Retreats."

5. Ibid.

6. Xi Jinping, "Speech."

7. Ibid.

8. Yu Xie, "China-Led Bank Spreads Its Wings."

9. Rasmus, "China's Bank and Waning US Hegemony."

10. "Data: Chinese Contracts in Africa"; "Data: Chinese Workers in Africa"; "Data: Chinese Foreign Aid."

11. Chuang, "No Way Forward," 205.

12. Ibid., 213.

13. Ibid., 208 (emphasis in original).

14. Ibid., 209.

15. Bulawayo, *We Need New Names*, 48.

16. Chuang, "No Way Forward," 208.

Bibliography

Ahmad, Aijaz. "Globalization and Culture." In *On Communalism and Globalization: Offensives of the Far Right*, 2nd ed., 93–117. New Delhi: Three Essays Collective, 2004.

Altbach, Philip G. "The Dilemma of Success: Universities in Advanced Developing Countries." *Prospects* 12, no. 3 (1982): 293–312.

Altbach, Philip G. "Key Issues of Textbook Provision in the Third World." *Prospects* 13, no. 3 (1983): 315–27.

Altbach, Philip G. "Literary Colonialism: Books in the Third World." *Harvard Educational Review* 45, no. 2 (July 1975): 226–36.

Altbach, Philip G. "Servitude of the Mind? Education, Dependency and Neocolonialism." *Teachers College Record* 79 (December 1977): 197–204.

Altbach, Philip G. "Third World Publishers and the International Knowledge System." *Logos* 2, no. 3 (1991): 122–26.

Altbach, Philip G. "The University as Center and Periphery." *Teachers College Record* 82 (Summer 1981): 601–21.

Altbach, Philip G., and Eva-Maria Rathgeber. *Publishing in the Third World: Trend Report and Bibliography*. New York: Praeger, 1980.

Apter, Andrew. *The Pan-African Nation: Oil and the Spectacle of Culture in Nigeria*. Chicago: University of Chicago Press, 2005.

Arnett, James. "Taking Pictures: The Economy of Affect and Postcolonial Performativity in NoViolet Bulawayo's *We Need New Names*." *ariel* 47, no. 3 (July 2016): 149–73.

Arrhe, M. "Great Literature of East and West." *UNESCO Courier* 6 (June 1957): 4–6.

Arrighi, Giovanni. *Adam Smith in Beijing: Lineages of the 21st Century*. London: Verso, 2009.

Arrighi, Giovanni. *The Long Twentieth Century: Money, Power and the Origins of Our Times*. London: Verso, 1994.

Barker, Ronald, and Robert Escarpit. "Copyright." In *The Book Hunger*, edited by Ronald Barker and Robert Escarpit, 88–102. Paris: UNESCO, 1973.

Barker, Ronald, and Robert Escarpit, eds. *The Book Hunger*. Paris: UNESCO, 1973.

Barnett, Stanley A., and Roland R. Piggford. *Manual on Book and Library Activities in Developing Countries*. Washington, DC: Agency for International Development, 1969.

Barnhisel, Greg. *Cold War Modernists: Art, Literature, and American Cultural Diplomacy*. New York: Columbia University Press, 2015.

Becker, Gary. *Human Capital: A Theoretical and Empirical Analysis, with Special Reference to Education*. Chicago: University of Chicago Press, 1964.

Beech, Dave. "Art and the Regime of Labour." *Historical Materialism*, forthcoming.

Behrstock, Julian. "UNESCO and the World of Books." *UNESCO Courier*, no. 9 (September 1965): 21–22.

Bell, David, and Kate Oakley. *Cultural Policy*. London: Routledge, 2014.

Benanav, Aaron, and John Clegg. "Misery and Debt: On the Logic and History of Surplus Population and Surplus Capital." In *Contemporary Marxist Theory*, edited by Andrew Pendakis et al., 585–608. New York: Bloomsbury, 2014.

Benjamin, Curtis. *U.S. Books Abroad: Neglected Ambassadors*. Washington, DC: Library of Congress, 1984.

Bennett, Eric. *Workshops of Empire: Stegner, Engle, and American Creative Writing During the Cold War*. Iowa: University of Iowa Press, 2015.

Besterman, Theodore. *Unesco: Peace in the Minds of Men*. London: Methuen & Co. Ltd., 1951.

Bgoya, Walter, and Mary Jay. "Publishing in Africa from Independence to the Present Day." *Research in African Literatures* 44, no. 2 (Summer 2013): 17–34.

Bokova, Irina. "The Power of Culture for Development." *Economic Cooperation and Development Review* (Feb 2013): 1–12.

Brattain, Michelle. "Race, Racism, and Antiracism: UNESCO and the Politics of Presenting Science to the Postwar Public." *The American Historical Review* 112, no. 5 (Dec 2007): 1386–413.

Brennan, Timothy. *Wars of Position: The Cultural Politics of Left and Right*. New York: Columbia University Press, 2007.

Brenner, Robert. *The Economics of Global Turbulence: The Advanced Capitalist Economies from Long Boom to Long Downturn, 1945–2005*. London: Verso, 2006.

Brouillette, Sarah, and David Thomas. "Forum: *Combined and Uneven Development*." Comparative Literature Studies 53, no. 3 (2016): 509–16.

Brown, Sidney Devere. "Yasunari Kawabata (1899–1972): Tradition versus Modernity." *World Literature Today* 62, no. 3 (Summer 1988): 375–79.

Bulawayo, NoViolet. *We Need New Names*. New York: Little, Brown & Co., 2013.

Cheah, Pheng. *What Is a World? On Postcolonial Literature as World Literature*. Durham: Duke University Press, 2016.

Chuang. "No Way Forward, No Way Back: China in the Era of Riots," *Chuang* 1 (2015): 191–227.

Clover, Joshua. "Fanon: Absorption and Coloniality." *College Literature* 45, no. 1 (2018): 39–45.

Clover, Joshua. *Riot. Strike. Riot: The New Era of Uprisings*. London: Verso, 2016.

Dangarembga, Tsitsi. *Nervous Conditions*. New York: Seal Press, 1988.

Darnton, Robert. "What Is the History of Books?" *Daedalus* 111, no. 3 (Summer 1982): 65–83.

"Data: Chinese Contracts in Africa." *China Africa Research Initiative*. http://www.sais -cari.org/data-chinese-contracts-in-africa/

"Data: Chinese Foreign Aid." *China Africa Research Initiative*. http://www.sais-cari.org/ data-chinese-foreign-aid-to-africa

"Data: Chinese Workers in Africa." *China Africa Research Initiative*. http://www.sais -cari.org/data-chinese-workers-in-africa

De Angelis, Massimo. "Neoliberal Governance, Reproduction and Accumulation." *The Commoner* 7 (Spring/Summer 2003): http://www.commoner.org.uk/07deangelis.doc

Doherty, Megan. "PEN International and Its Republic of Letters 1921–1970." PhD diss., Columbia University, 2011.

Dorn, Charles, and Kristen Ghodsee. "The Cold War Politicization of Literacy: Communism, UNESCO, and the World Bank." *Diplomatic History* 36, no. 3 (April 2012): 373–98.

"Dublin UNESCO City of Literature." City of Dublin, 2009. http://www.dublincityof literature.net/wp-content/uploads/Dublin-UNESCO-Bid.pdf

Ede, Amatoritsero. "Narrative Moment and Self-Anthropologizing Discourse." *Research in African Literatures* 46, no. 3 (Fall 2015): 112–29.

Emre, Merve. *Paraliterary: The Making of Bad Readers in Postwar America*. Chicago: University of Chicago Press, 2017.

Endnotes. "A History of Separation." *Endnotes* 4 (2015): 70–192.

Escarpit, Robert. *The Book Revolution*. London: Harrap, 1966.

Federici, Silvia. *Caliban and the Witch*. New York: Autonomedia, 2004.

Ferguson, Karen. *Top Down: The Ford Foundation, Black Power, and the Reinvention of Racial Liberalism*. Philadelphia: University of Pennsylvania Press, 2013.

Finn, Chester. "How to Lose the War of Ideas." *Commentary* 76, no. 2 (August 1983): 41–50.

Fourth Conference of Heads of State or Government of Non-Aligned Countries. Algiers, 1973. New York: United Nations, 1973.

Franssen, Thomas, and Giselinde Kuipers. "Sociology of Literature and Publishing in the Early 21st Century: Away From the Centre." *Cultural Sociology* 9, no. 3 (2015): 291–95.

Fraser, Nancy. "Expropriation and Exploitation in Racialized Capitalism: A Reply to Michael Dawson." *Critical Historical Studies* (Spring 2016): 163–78.

Giffard, C. Anthony. *UNESCO and the Media*. New York: Addison-Wesley Longman, 1989.

Gilman, Nils. *Mandarins of the Future: Modernization Theory in Cold War America*. Baltimore, MD: Johns Hopkins University Press, 2003.

Griswold, Wendy. *Regionalism and the Reading Class*. Chicago: University of Chicago Press, 2007.

Hall, Stuart, et al. *Policing the Crisis: Mugging, the State, and Law and Order*. London: Macmillan, 1978.

Harris, Ashleigh. "Hot Reads, Pirate Copies, and the Unsustainability of the Book in Africa's Literary Future." *Postcolonial Text*, forthcoming.

Hazzard, Anthony. *Postwar Anti-Racism: The United States, UNESCO, and "Race,"* 1945– 1968. London: Palgrave, 2012.

Hewison, Robert. *Culture and Consensus: England, Art and Politics since 1940*. London: Methuen, 1995.

Hoveyda, Fereydoun. *Dans une terre étrange*. Paris: Gallimard, 1967.

Hoveyda, Fereydoun. *Les Quarantaines*. Paris: Gallimard, 1962.

Huxley, Julian. "Colonies and Freedom." *The New Republic* 24 (January 1944): 106–8.

Huxley, Julian. *UNESCO: Its Purpose and Philosophy*. New York: Public Affairs Press, 1948.

Huxley, Julian, with Phyllis Deane. *The Future of the Colonies*. London: Pilot Press, 1944.

Huxley, Julian, A. C. Haddon, and A. M. Carr-Saunders. *We Europeans: A Survey of "Racial" Problems*. London: Jonathan Cape, 1935.

Ikheloa, Ikhide. "The 2011 Caine Prize: How Not to Write About Africa." *NEXT Magazine*, May 2011. https://xokigbo.com/2012/03/11/the-2011-caine-prize-how-not-to -write-about-africa/

Julien, Eileen. "The Extroverted African Novel." In *The Novel, Volume 1: History, Geography and Culture*, edited by Franco Moretti et al., 667–702. Princeton: Princeton University Press, 2007.

Kawabata, Yasunari. *Snow Country*. Translated by Edward Seidensticker. New York: Alfred A. Knopf, 1956.

Klein, Christina. *Cold War Orientalism: Asia in the Middlebrow Imagination*, 1945– 1981. Berkeley: University of California Press, 2003.

Kotei, S. I. A. *The Book Today in Africa*. Paris: UNESCO, 1981.

"Krakow City of Literature." http://miastoliteratury.pl/wp-content/uploads/2013/07/ Krakow_UNESCO_EN.pdf

Laves, Walter. *UNESCO and Economic Development*. Washington, DC: U.S. National Commission for UNESCO, 1953.

Leary, John Pat. "Innovation and the Neoliberal Idioms of Development." *boundary2* (2 August 2018): http://www.boundary2.org/2018/08/leary/

Lewis, Justin, and Toby Miller. "Introduction." In *Critical Cultural Policy Studies: A Reader*, edited by Justin Lewis and Toby Miller, 1–10. Oxford: Blackwell, 2002.

Litt, Paul. *The Muses, the Masses, and the Massey Commission*. Toronto: University of Toronto Press, 1992.

Lynch, Colum, and Elias Groll. "As U.S. Retreats From World Organizations, China Steps In to Fill the Void." *Foreign Policy* (6 October, 2017). https://foreignpolicy.com/2017/10 /06/as-u-s-retreats-from-world-organizations-china-steps-in-the-fill-the-void/

Matsugu, Miho. "In the Service of the Nation: Geishi and Kawabata Yasunari's *Snow Country*." In *The Courtesan's Arts: Cross-Cultural Perspectives*, edited by Martha Feldman and Bonnie Gordon, 243–52. Oxford: Oxford University Press, 2006.

Matsugu, Miho. "The War in Kawabata Yasunari's *Snow Country*: Aesthetics of Empire, Politics of Literature, Struggle of Women." PhD diss., University of Chicago, 2005.

Mazower, Mark. *Governing the World: The History of an Idea*. New York: Penguin Press, 2012.

McCarthy, Kathleen. "From Cold War to Cultural Development: The International Cultural Activities of the Ford Foundation, 1950–1980." *Daedalus* 116.1 (Winter 1987): 93–117.

McNally, David. "From Financial Crisis to World-Slump: Accumulation, Financialisation, and the Global Slowdown." *Historical Materialism* 17 (2009): 35–83.

Mda, Zakes. *The Heart of Redness*. New York: Farrar, Straus, and Giroux, 2000.

Mda, Zakes. *When People Play People: Development Communication Through Theatre*. London: Zed Books, 1993.

Midnight Notes Collective. "Introduction to the New Enclosures." *Midnight Notes* 10, (1990). http://www.midnightnotes.org/pdfnewenc1.pdf

Mikić, Hristina. *Measuring the Economic Contribution of Cultural Industries: A Review and Assessment of Current Methodological Approaches*. Montreal: UNESCO Institute for Statistics, 2012.

Mileva, Leda. "UNESCO and World Literary Values." In *Translators and Their Position in Society*, 97–104. Vienna: Braumueller, 1985.

Miller, Toby, Victoria Durrer, and Dave O'Brien. *The Routledge Handbook of Global Cultural Policy*. Abingdon: Routledge, 2018.

Miller, Toby, and George Yúdice. *Cultural Policy*. London: Sage, 2002.

Offe, Claus. *Contradictions of the Welfare State*. Edited by John Keane. London: Hutchison, 1984.

Österling, Anders. "Award Ceremony Speech. Nobel Prize in Literature 1968: Yasunari Kawabata." *Nobelprize.org*. Nobel Media AB, 2014. https://www.nobelprize.org/nobel_prizes/literature/laureates/1968/press.html

Perry, Rachel E. "Immutable Mobiles: UNESCO's Archives of Colour Reproductions." *The Art Bulletin* 99, no. 2 (2017): 166–85.

Prashad, Vijay. *The Darker Nations: A People's History of the Third World*. New York: The New Press, 2007.

Rangil, Teresa Tomas. "The Politics of Neutrality: UNESCO's Social Science Department, 1946–1956." *CHOPE Working Paper*, no. 2011–08 (April 2011).

Rasmus, Jack. "China's Bank and Waning US Hegemony." *Counterpunch* (30 March 2015). https://www.counterpunch.org/2015/03/30/chinas-bank-waning-usa-hegemony/

Ravelonanosy, George. "New Copyright Revision Means More Books for the Third World." *UNESCO Courier*, no. 7 (July 1972): 32.

Richards, Pamela Spence. "The Soviet Overseas Information Empire and the Implications of Its Disintegration." In *Proceedings of the 1998 Conference on the History and Heritage of Science Information Systems*, edited by M. E. Bowden, T. B. Hahn, and R. V. Williams, 201–14. Medford, NJ: Information Today for the American Society for Information Science and the Chemical Heritage Foundation, 1999.

Rist, Gilbert. *The History of Development: From Western Origins to Global Faith*, 4th ed. London: Zed Books, 2014.

Rosenstein, Carole. *Understanding Cultural Policy*. Abingdon: Routledge, 2018.

Rostow, W. W. *The Stages of Economic Growth: A Non-Communist Manifesto*. Cambridge: Cambridge University Press, 1960.

Saikawa, Takashi. "Returning to the International Community: UNESCO and Postwar Japan, 1945–1951." In *A History of UNESCO: Global Actions and Impacts*, edited by Paul Duedahl, 116–30. London: Palgrave, 2016.

Salih, Tayeb. "The Doum Tree of Wad Hamid." In *The Wedding of Zein and Other Stories*. London: Heinemann, 1968.

Saunders, Frances Stonor. *Who Paid the Piper? The CIA and the Cultural Cold War*. London: Granta, 1999.

Schiller, Herb. "Decolonization of Information: Efforts Toward a New International Order." *Latin American Perspectives* 5 (1978): 35–48.

Schlesinger, Arthur M., Jr. *The Vital Center: The Politics of Freedom*. 1949. Reprint, Boston: Houghton Mifflin Company, 1962.

Schlesinger, Philip. "The Creative Economy: Invention of a Global Orthodoxy." *Innovation* 30, no. 1 (2017): 73–90.

Schryer, Stephen. *Maximum Feasible Participation: American Literature and the War on Poverty*. Stanford: Stanford University Press, 2018.

Schwartz, Lawrence H. *Creating Faulkner's Reputation: The Politics of Modern Literary Criticism*. Knoxville: University of Tennessee Press, 1988.

Sewell, James Patrick. *UNESCO and World Politics: Engaging in International Relations*. Princeton: Princeton University Press, 1975.

Slaughter, Joseph. *Human Rights Inc.: The World Novel, Narrative Form, and International Law*. New York: Fordham University Press, 2007.

Sluga, Glenda. "UNESCO and the (One) World of Julian Huxley." *Journal of World History* 21, no. 3 (Sept 2010): 393–418.

Smith, John. "Imperialism in the Twenty-First Century." *Monthly Review* 67, no. 3 (July–August 2015). https://monthlyreview.org/2015/07/01/imperialism-in-the-twenty-first-century/

Smith, Keith B. *The Impact of Transnational Book Publishing on Intellectual Knowledge in Less Developed Countries*. Paris: UNESCO, 1977.

Smith, Roger. "Biology and Values in Interwar Britain: C. S. Sherrington, Julian Huxley and the Vision of Progress." *Past & Present* 178 (Feb 2003): 210–42.

Staunton, Irene. "Publishing for Pleasure in Zimbabwe: The Experience of Weaver Press." *Wasafiri* 31, no. 4 (December 2016): 49–54.

Strauhs, Doreen. *African Literary NGOs: Power, Politics, and Participation*. London: Palgrave, 2013.

"Toward a New World Order." *UNESCO Courier*, no. 3 (March 1977): 4.

Travis, Trysh. "Middlebrow Culture in the Cold War: Books USA Advertisements, 1967." *PMLA* 128, no. 2 (2013): 468–73.

Truman, Harry S. "Inaugural Address." Washington, DC, 20 January 1949. The American Presidency Project. https://www.presidency.ucsb.edu/node/229929

Tzouvala, Konstantina. "Letters of Blood and Fire: A Socio-Economic History of International Law." PhD diss., Durham Law School, Durham University, 2016.

UNCTAD, UNDP, UNESCO, WIPO, ITC. *Creative Economy Report. The Challenge of Assessing the Creative Economy: Towards Informed Policy-Making.* Geneva, 2008.

UNESCO. *Anatomy of an International Year: Book Year—1972, Reports and Papers on Communication 71.* Paris: UNESCO, 1974.

UNESCO. *Books for All: A Programme of Action.* Paris: UNESCO, 1973.

UNESCO. "Charter of the Book." *UNESCO Bulletin for Libraries* 26, vol. 5 (1972): 238–41.

UNESCO. "Constitution." *unesco.org* (16 Nov 1945). http://portal.unesco.org/en/ev.php-URL_ID=15244&URL_DO=DO_TOPIC&URL_SECTION=201.html

UNESCO. "Convention on the Protection and Promotion of the Diversity of Cultural Expressions." Paris: UNESCO, 2005. http://portal.unesco.org/en/ev.php-URL_ID=31038&URL_DO=DO_TOPIC&URL_SECTION=201.html

UNESCO. "Copyright: A Lifeline to the Zimbabwe Book Industry." *unesco.org* (20 Apr 2017). https://en.unesco.org/creativity/news/copyright-lifeline-zimbabwe-book-industry

UNESCO. "Creative Cities Network, 2017 Call for Applications: Applicant's Handbook." Paris: UNESCO, 2017.

UNESCO. *Cultural Policy: A Preliminary Study.* Studies and Documents on Cultural Policies. Paris: UNESCO, 1969.

UNESCO. "Declaration on Fundamental Principles Concerning the Contribution of the Mass Media to Strengthening Peace and International Understanding, to the Promotion of Human Rights and to Countering Racialism, Apartheid and Incitement to War." In "Records of the General Conference, Twentieth Session, Resolutions," 100–104. Paris: UNESCO, 1978.

UNESCO. "Developing a National Strategy on Copyright." https://en.unesco.org/creativity/ifcd/projects/developing-national-strategy-copyright

UNESCO. *The Experimental World Literacy Programme: A Critical Assessment.* Paris: UNESCO, 1976.

UNESCO. *The Experimental World Literacy Programme and Its Global Evaluation: Interim Report.* Paris: UNESCO, 1974.

UNESCO. *Intergovernmental Conference on Cultural Policies in Africa.* Paris: UNESCO, 1975.

UNESCO. *International Fund for Cultural Diversity, 2014 Report.* Paris: UNESCO, 2014.

UNESCO. *Many Voices, One World.* Paris: UNESCO, 1980.

UNESCO. "Measuring the Economic Contribution of Cultural Industries." https://en.unesco.org/creativity/ifcd/projects/measuring-economic-contribution-cultural

UNESCO. *Medium-Term Plan (1977–1982).* Paris: UNESCO, 1976.

UNESCO. "Records of the General Conference, Paris 1964: Thirteenth Session, Resolutions." Paris: UNESCO, 1964.

UNESCO. *Report of the Director General on the Activities of the Organization,* 1954. Paris: UNESCO, 1955.

UNESCO. "Report of UNESCO to the Economic and Social Council of the United Nations on the Translation of the Classics." Paris: UNESCO, 1948.

UNESCO. *UNESCO Collection of Representative Works,* 1948–2000. Paris: UNESCO, 2000.

UNESCO. *World Conference on Cultural Policies: Final Report.* Paris: UNESCO, 1982.

United Nations. "Charter of the United Nations." http://www.un.org/en/sections/un -charter/un-charter-full-text/

United Nations Economic and Social Council. "Resolutions Adopted by the Economic and Social Council during Its Fourth Session." *un.org,* Resolution 53, no. 4 (28 March 1947). http://dag.un.org/handle/11176/399463[0]

United Nations General Assembly. "Declaration on the Establishment of a New International Economic Order." *UN Documents,* 1974. www.un-documents.net/s6r3201.htm

United Nations General Assembly. "Resolutions Adopted by the General Assembly during Its First Session." *un.org,* Resolution 60, no. 1 (14 December 1946). www .un.org/documents/ga/res/1/ares1.htm

Walker, Larry. "Unbinding the Japanese Novel in English Translation: The Alfred A. Knopf Program, 1955–1977." PhD diss., University of Helsinki, 2015.

Wallerstein, Immanuel. "Modernization: Requiescat in Pace." 1976. Reprinted in *The Capitalist World-Economy,* 132–37. Cambridge: Cambridge University Press, 1979.

Warwick Research Collective. *Combined and Uneven Development: Towards a New Theory of World-Literature.* Liverpool: Liverpool University Press, 2015.

Warwick Research Collective. "WReC's Reply." *Comparative Literature Studies* 53, no. 3 (2016): 535–49.

Wells, Clare. *The UN, UNESCO, and the Politics of Knowledge.* New York: Macmillan, 1987.

Westall, Claire, and Michael Gardiner. *The Public on the Public: The British Public as Trust, Reflexivity and Political Foreclosure.* London: Palgrave, 2014.

Wirtén, Eva Hemmungs. *Cosmopolitan Copyright: Law and Language in the Translation Zone.* Uppsala: Uppsala University, 2011.

Xi Jinping. "Speech by H. E. Xi Jinping President of the People's Republic of China At UNESCO Headquarters." Paris, 27 March 2014. http://www.unesco.org/new/ fileadmin/MULTIMEDIA/HQ/ERI/pdf/Speech_Xi_Jinping_English.pdf

Yúdice, George. *The Expediency of Culture: Uses of Culture in the Global Era.* Durham, NC: Duke University Press, 2004.

Yúdice, George. "The Privatization of Culture." *Social Text* 59 (summer 1999): 17–34.

Yu Xie. "China-Led Bank Spreads Its Wings to Africa, South America to Bankroll Infrastructure Projects." *South China Morning Post* (16 Jan 2018). http://www .scmp.com/business/banking-finance/article/2128343/china-led-bank-spreads-its -yuan-africa-south-america

Index

Accra, 60, 87–89
activism, 133, 137
Africa, 16; cultures of, 55, 60, 87, 117;
    development of, 30–31, 85, 89, 133,
    145–46; and diamond mining, 125,
    134–37; literature of, 95, 123–25,
    128, 131, 137. *See also* agriculture;
    aid; book donation schemes; book
    industries; Britain; capitalism; China;
    colonization; developing world;
    development; developmentalism;
    economies; imperialism;
    industrialization; racism; resources;
    tourism; United States; urbanization
African Books Collective (ABC), 127–28
African Publishers Network, 128
African Study Meeting on Copyright,
    131
agriculture, 31, 34, 62, 64, 67,
    100, 115, 118, 133, 145. *See
    also* Africa; aid; employment;
    heritage; industrialization; labor;
    modernization
Ahmad, Aijaz, 140
aid, 7, 32, 89, 113, 120, 128, 133, 143–
    44. *See also* Africa; book donation
    schemes; Britain; economies;
    International Monetary Fund (IMF);
    marketization; nongovernmental
    organizations (NGOs); trade; United
    States; World Bank

Algeria, 58
Algiers Conference of the Heads of State
    of the Non-Aligned Countries, 91
Algiers Programme of Action, 91
Altbach, Philip, 79, 89–90, 153n3
Americanization, 52–53, 59, 139
Amnesty International, 93
Anand, Mulk Raj, 55
Arabic (language), 21, 25, 69
Arnett, James, 133
Arrighi, Giovanni, 14, 83, 149n1
art, 3, 5, 8–9, 28, 39–40, 48–50, 56–57,
    102
Arts Council of Great Britain, 12
Asian Infrastructure Investment Bank
    (AIIB), 145
The Atlantic, 44
Avicenna, 25
A Winter's Tale (Shakespeare), 25
"Ayame" (Strauss), 44

Baghdad, 102
Balibar, Étienne, 5, 8
Balibar, Renée, 5, 8
Balkans, 112
ballet, 46–50, 53
Bandung Asian-African Conference, 85
Barker, Ronald, 89
Barnhisel, Greg, 8
Beijing, 147
Benjamin, Curtis, 95

Bennett, Eric, 8

Berne Convention for the Protection of Literary and Artistic Works, 81, 126, 131

Bgoya, Walter, 125–27

biological determinism, 27, 35–36. *See also* race

Black Arts movements, 9, 16

black empowerment, 116, 121, 134

Blum, Léon, 31

The Bodley Head (publisher), 25

Bogota, 88

Bokova, Irina, 114

book donation schemes, 14, 90, 92, 94–95, 126

book hunger, 1–2, 14, 77–97, 108, 131

The Book Hunger (Barker and Escarpit), 13–14, 89

book industries: challenges of, 89, 91–92, 97, 102, 128; growth of, 81, 87–88, 103, 123–26, 131–32; indigenous, 79, 89, 92; literary, 3, 19, 24, 28–29, 108; power of, 80, 90, 97, 104. *See also* publishing industries; resources

books: access to, 1–2, 102–8, 129, 141; exportation of, 77–97; as indoctrination, 95; as tools, 10–14, 97. *See also* literature; media; publishing industries

Books for All, 90

Books for the Developing Countries, 88, 90

Books USA, 95

The Book Today in Africa (Kotei), 90

Bourdieu, Pierre, 8, 55

branding, 1, 11, 17, 103–5, 108, 141, 147. *See also* capitalism; City of Literature; culture; heritage; marketization; tourism

Brattain, Michelle, 35

Brenner, Robert, 149n1

Britain: colonization and, 30–32, 34–35, 120, 134; hegemony of, 10, 12, 14, 92; publishing in, 69, 125–27, 130; UNESCO and, 94, 97, 145. *See also* colonization; Euro-centrism; Europe; imperialism

British Colonial Development and Welfare Act, 31

British Council, 81

British High Commission, 94

British South Africa Company, 134

Brown, Sidney Devere, 40, 51

Budding Writers Association of Zimbabwe, 128

Bulawayo, NoViolet, 18, 124, 132–42

Bullis, Harry A., 42–43

Caine Prize for African Writing, 124–25, 134, 137

Cairo, 88

Caliban and the Witch (Federici), 72

capitalism: democracy and, 42, 99, 139; development and, 2, 10, 67, 100, 125; free market, 13, 81–82, 103; growth of, 11, 14–15, 34, 60, 68, 72, 95, 146; humanization of, 53, 56, 65; incorporation and, 6, 13–14, 101, 113, 140; individualism and, 40, 140; industrialization and, 50, 52, 96; opposition to, 3–5, 7, 69; power of, 5, 8–9, 30, 78, 83, 90. *See also* Britain; colonization; economies; employment; extraction; imperialism; industrialization; labor; marketization; technology; unemployment; United States; urbanization; wealth

Cassin, René, 57–58

censorship, 143–44

charity, 133–36, 143

Charter of Economic Rights and Duties of States, 140

Charter of the Book, 78, 82, 86, 89, 92

Cheah, Pheng, 3–4, 6–7

Chijimi cloth, 48–50, 53, 142

Chilongo, Green Kephas, 130

China, 47, 143–44, 146–47

Chuang Collective, 146–47

City of Literature, 11, 18, 102–5, 108, 121

Cold War, 8–9, 39, 42, 61, 81, 90

Collection of Representative Works, 10, 21–37, 40–41, 44, 51, 77, 87–88, 139–40

"Colonies and Freedom" (Huxley), 30

colonization: history of, 4, 8, 60, 91, 93, 115, 120, 125, 127, 133–34, 136–37; literary, 31, 89–90, 129–30; new, 30, 34, 141, 156n26; power of, 6, 10, 14, 33, 36, 118–19. *See also* Britain; capitalism; developing world; economies; exploitation; imperialism; industrialization; racism; United States

Columbia University Press, 25

commercialization, 6, 51, 59

commodification, 6–7, 68–69, 141

communications industry, 1, 4, 13, 29, 78–79, 81, 85, 91–92, 96–97, 114, 141–42

communism, 10, 39–40, 63, 66, 92, 94–95

community, 11, 13, 25–34, 40, 51, 72–74, 79–84, 95, 115–19, 128–30, 139–42

Congress for Cultural Freedom, 12

conscientization, 32, 41, 120

consumerism, 18, 43, 79, 82–87, 106

Convention on the Protection and Promotion of the Diversity of Cultural Expressions (2005), 108–11

cooperative enterprise, 78, 114–20, 142

copyright law, 1, 7, 18–19, 77, 89–90, 100, 123–37, 153n10

corporatism, 86, 144–47

cosmopolitanism, 1, 11–12, 29, 58. *See also* liberalism

cottage industries, 116, 120

Creative and Cultural Industries (CCIs), 130

Creative Cities Network, 1, 11, 102, 108, 141

creative economies, 10–11, 15, 17–18, 101, 103, 105, 110, 122–23, 129, 141, 147

culture: authenticity of, 38, 47, 60, 68, 105; branding of, 10, 16–17, 25, 47, 51, 121; commercialization of, 107, 142; definitions of, 6; destruction of, 7, 15, 41, 51, 62; development of, 13, 28–33, 56–66, 74, 78, 99–106, 121; diversity and, 35, 51, 53, 108, 112–13; economics of, 2, 11–12, 16, 22, 59, 101, 111, 130; employment and, 17, 119, 121; exportation of, 8–9, 34, 57, 61; humanization and, 67, 75, 141; indigenous, 6, 8, 21, 60, 88; literary, 1–8, 12, 39, 45, 51–60, 79, 103–8, 128, 137, 141; nationalism and, 13, 23, 52; preservation of, 49; production of, 2, 6, 10, 16, 18, 48, 110, 140; resiliency and, 9, 114, 141; value of, 15, 23–24, 32, 66, 100, 109, 111. *See also* branding; development; heritage; tourism

Culture for Development Indicators (CDIS), 111

Czechoslovakia, 87–88

Dangarembga, Tsitsi, 134

Dans une terre étrange (Hoveyda), 58

Darnton, Robert, 79–82, 97

Deane, Phyllis, 30–32

debt, 56, 96, 99, 121, 145–46

decolonization, 1, 14–16, 82, 90

democracy, 8, 11, 15, 41, 43

dependency theory, 83, 90, 120

developing world: capitalism and the, 3, 141, 145; colonization and the, 26–27, 32–33, 45, 122–23; conditions of the, 1, 4, 10–11, 13–14, 16, 33; incorporation of the, 6, 10, 15, 18, 27, 108, 110–12; industrialization and the, 79, 83–101, 126, 132; policy and the, 12, 59–65, 140; technology and the, 43, 58. *See also*

Africa; aid; capitalism; economies;
Euro-centrism; Europe; imperialism;
industrialization; marketization;
resources; technology; tourism
development: benefits of, 114, 116, 121;
cooperative, 73, 117; economics
of, 10, 13, 22; endogenous, 83–84;
forms of, 16, 84, 89, 111, 120; global,
33, 85; guidelines of, 99–100, 112;
humanization of, 13, 15, 27, 63,
68, 114, 119–20; inevitability of,
71, 74, 122, 142; theory, 3, 65, 72,
75, 85, 113, 121, 135, 145; uneven,
3, 67, 102–3. *See also* capitalism;
economies; industrialization;
marketization; technology
developmentalism: economic, 15,
74, 141; opposition to, 66, 72,
118; theories of, 27, 31, 53, 56,
62–63, 83; UNESCO and, 14, 36,
42; United States and, 60–61. *See
also* economies; Euro-centrism;
imperialism; industrialization;
marketization; trade
Discours de la méthode (Descartes), 25
Divine Comedy (Dante), 25
Doherty, Megan, 42
Dorn, Charles, 65
"The Doum Tree of Wad Hamid" (Salih),
13, 69–73, 113, 142
Dublin, 102, 104

East African Literature Bureau, 126
*The Economics of Book Publishing in
Developing Countries* (Smith Jr.), 90
economies: books and, 79–80, 82, 95;
conditions of, 1, 8, 18, 27, 61, 108,
139; crises of, 2, 10, 12–13, 56,
66–67, 83, 99, 121, 126–27, 133, 140;
culture and, 2, 101, 103, 140, 147;
development and, 10, 13, 53, 59, 64,
82, 88, 142; dynamic, 3, 9, 11–12, 45,
122, 139, 141, 145; global, 16–17,
33–34, 65, 72; governance and, 43,
89, 112, 146; humanization of, 62,

114, 141; integration of, 42, 56, 60,
66, 69, 136, 142; intellectual, 96, 106;
trade and, 14, 16, 43; underdeveloped,
65, 67, 94, 132, 137; urban, 103;
vulnerability of, 118, 149n1. *See
also* colonization; developing world;
development; developmentalism;
employment; extraction;
industrialization; labor; resources;
tourism; trade; United States
ecotourism, 114–19. *See also* tourism
Edinburgh, 102
education, 12, 29, 31–32, 36, 58, 62–65,
77, 102, 125, 127, 134–36. *See also*
colonization; development; Euro-
centrism; imperialism; textbooks;
universities
Egypt, 58
Eisenhower, Dwight D., 8
Emerson, Rupert, 83
employment: lack of, 17, 63, 67, 128;
opportunities, 12, 66, 101, 104–5,
111, 115; promises of, 128, 136;
and resilience, 116, 120; writing as,
134, 136–37. *See also* capitalism;
developing world; economies; labor;
unemployment; wealth
Emre, Merve, 8
Endnotes research collective, 149n1
English (language), 21–25, 34, 37, 44,
69, 88–89, 95, 124, 139, 142
Escarpit, Robert, 14, 88–89
Essays (Bacon), 25
Euro-centrism, 32–33, 78, 80–83, 85–86,
90–92, 97, 134–36, 140. *See also*
capitalism; colonization; education;
imperialism; racism; wealth
Europe, 7, 11, 34–38, 55–58, 81–89, 104,
115–18, 124–31, 137–45
Experimental World Literacy Program
(EWLP), 63–65
exploitation, 10, 16, 43, 52, 68, 72,
83, 99–100, 135–37, 143–46. *See
also* employment; labor; racism;
resources; tourism

expropriation, 4, 16, 30, 140. *See also* colonization; culture; Euro-centrism; racism

extraction, 4, 7, 100. *See also* capitalism; colonization; economies; Euro-centrism; industrialization; labor; racism; resources

fascism, 10, 27

Faulkner, William, 39

Febvre, Lucien, 78–79

Ferguson, Karen, 9

Ford Foundation, 9, 12, 38, 62, 81, 127

Foreign Policy, 143

Foucault, Michel, 9

The Four Stages of Growth (Rostow), 63

France, 10, 31, 34, 57–58

Franco, Jean, 8

Fraser, Nancy, 16

freedom, 8, 12, 15, 30, 40–42, 60, 93–95, 99, 107–9, 118, 142

French (language), 21, 24–25, 34, 46, 88, 139

French Ministry of Culture, 81

The Future of the Colonies (Huxley and Deane), 29–30, 33

García Canclini, Néstor, 6

Gaulle, Charles de, 57

geisha, 46–48, 50, 53, 142

General Agreement on Tariffs and Trade (GATT), 101

Ghana Association of Writers, 90

Al-Ghazali, 25

Ghodsee, Kristen, 65

Gilman, Nils, 83

globalism, 40, 44, 74

globalization, 3, 5, 50, 110

global south. *See* developing world

Goldmann, Lucien, 8

governance, 2–3, 9, 15–17, 56, 67–73, 82, 99–103, 109, 114–19, 121, 126, 141, 149n1. *See also* policy making; politics

Grove Press, 25

Guatemala, 112

Haddon, A. C., 35

Hall, Stuart, 8

The Heart of Redness (Mda), 18, 114–22, 142

heritage: branding of, 1, 11, 15–16, 18, 141; preservation of, 13, 26, 29, 38, 49, 51, 58, 106, 114–19, 142, 147. *See also* culture; development; tourism

"Hitting Budapest" (Bulawayo), 134

Hoggart, Richard, 8, 55

Hoveyda, Fereydoun, 57

"How Not to Write About Africa" (Ikheloa), 134

Human Capital (Becker), 62

humanism, 35, 41–42, 51–53, 68, 141. *See also* transhumanism

humanitarianism, 7, 82, 133–46

human rights, 1, 62–63, 86, 92

Human Rights Inc. (Slaughter), 82

Hussein, Taha, 23

Huxley, Julian, 11, 26, 28–33, 35–36, 41

Ikheloa, Ikhide, 134

illiteracy, 1, 31, 43, 63–67, 77, 82, 127. *See also* literacy

imperialism: cultural, 13, 91, 141; economics of, 6, 10, 65, 100, 134; legacies of, 85, 140; new, 31–34, 83, 100, 139; Western, 4, 27, 47, 96. *See also* Britain; colonization; developing world; economies; education; Euro-centrism; Europe; expropriation; extraction; racism; technology; tourism; United States; wealth

inclusivity, 11, 40, 50, 81, 103–8, 119, 136, 144. *See also* development; economies

Index Translationum, 77

India, 87, 91

India: Matri Bhumi (film), 58

industrialization, 40, 50–52, 64, 88, 140, 145–46

infrastructure, 4–5, 17, 24, 36, 62, 81,
    85, 96, 101–3, 116–20, 133, 139–45
Intangible Cultural Heritage, 26
integration, 9–15, 50, 56, 60, 64–73,
    140–42
intellectual property, 2, 16–17, 97–100,
    110–13, 126–31
Intergovernmental Conference on
    Cultural Policies in Africa, 60
International Booksellers Federation,
    102
International Book Year, 10, 13, 77–78,
    86–87, 90, 92
International Commission for the
    Translation of Great Books, 25
International Commission on the
    History of Literature, 23
International Committee for
    Translations, 24
International Council of Scientific
    Unions, 23
International Federation of Library
    Associations and Institutions, 102
International Fund for Cultural Diversity
    (IFCD), 111–13, 121, 123, 130
International House, 38
International Institute of Philosophy, 23
internationalism, 36, 41–44, 58, 142
International Monetary Fund (IMF), 72,
    99, 145
International Publishers Association,
    81, 102
International Reading Association, 90
International Social Science, 8
International Standard Book Number
    (ISBN), 77
International Union for the History of
    Science, 23
investments, 11, 16, 32, 36, 43, 50,
    60–66, 104, 108, 121–33, 140–45.
    See also aid; capitalism; economies;
    extraction; wealth
Iowa City, 102
Iran, 57–58
Islam, 70

Japan, 37–38, 43–52, 89, 142, 145
Jay, Mary, 125–26
Johnson, Lyndon B., 9

Karachi, 87
Kawabata, Yasunari, 11, 37–39, 41–42,
    44, 48, 51–52, 59
Keene, Donald, 44
Keynes, John Maynard, 12
Kiku, Kodaka, 48
Klein, Christina, 44
Knopf, Alfred A., 12, 25, 37–38
knowledge, 11, 21, 26–34, 64–67, 78,
    82, 88–95, 105–9, 121, 132. *See also*
    Euro-centrism; illiteracy; languages;
    literacy; science; technology;
    textbooks; universities
Kotei, S. I. A., 90
Krakow, 102–7

labor: exploitation of, 72, 113, 137;
    mobility of, 73, 100, 111, 115,
    118, 122, 124, 133, 135, 152n10;
    training and, 99, 140, 147, 149n1;
    value of, 62, 128, 146–47. *See also*
    capitalism; colonization; developing
    world; economies; employment;
    imperialism; technology; trade;
    unemployment; wealth
Lane, Alan, 23
languages, 21–22, 24, 29. *See also* Arabic
    (language); English (language);
    French (language); Portuguese
    (language); Spanish (language)
L'Apparition du livre (Febvre & Martin),
    79
Laves, Walter, 42–43
Leary, John Pat, 141
Lebanon, 21, 25
legitimation processes, 4, 68, 86, 90, 109.
    See also inclusivity
Lesotho, 114, 120
Les Quarantaines (Hoveyda), 58
liberalism, 2, 9–11, 40, 44, 139. *See
    also* Britain; capitalism; economies;

Europe; governance; trade; United States
libraries, 24, 87, 102, 104, 125, 127, 131
literacy, 31, 43, 62–66, 70–71, 81–83, 88, 103, 109, 125–29. *See also* book donation schemes; book industries; illiteracy; knowledge; publishing industries; technology
literary industries. *See* book industries
literature: anti-political, 39–41, 45, 50–51, 142; audiences of, 3, 120, 124–25, 128–29, 132, 134, 136; classic, 21–23; decline of, 2, 6, 18, 105, 108, 121–22, 128–29, 137, 141; governance and, 1–3, 9–12, 78; histories of, 11, 26, 77, 81–82; Japanese, 37–38; scholarship and, 1–2, 4–5, 7–8, 79, 97, 104; wealth and, 1, 6, 8, 28. *See also* book industries; English (language); French (language); illiteracy; literacy; translation; universities; *specific programs; specific works*
localism, 18, 29, 74. *See also* cooperative enterprise; governance; heritage
London, 125, 127
Lower Telle Beekeepers Collective Trust, 119–20
Lukács, Georg, 8

MacBride, Séan, 93
MacBride Commission, 93
Macherey, Pierre, 5, 8
MacLeish, Archibald, 11
Macmillan (publisher), 25
Made to Measure (Pellowski), 90
Maheu, René, 56–57, 59, 63, 88
Makore, Samuel, 129
Malraux, André, 57
marketization, 2, 6–7, 72, 81, 92, 99–103, 109–12, 125, 127. *See also* capitalism; development; economies; labor; technology; urbanization; wealth
Martin, Henri-Jean, 79

Marxism, 3, 8
Mass Media Declaration, 92–93
Matsugu, Miho, 38
Matsumoto, Shigeharu, 38
M'Bow, Amadou-Mahtar, 6, 56, 59, 68, 84
McCarthy, Kathleen, 61
McGraw-Hill, 95
McNally, David, 99
McNamara, Robert, 62–63
Mda, Zakes, 18, 114–19, 121–22
media: indigenous, 91, 112; new, 85, 88, 102, 104, 106, 120, 125; policy and, 91, 94, 109; poverty and, 14, 133–34, 140; risks of, 56, 59; technology and, 106, 110; as tool, 133, 135–36. *See also* development; globalism; marketization; technology; tourism
Medium-Term Plan (UNESCO), 83
Melbourne, 102
Melcher, Frederic, 23
Mexico, 25
Mexico City Declaration on Cultural Policies, 55, 67–68
Midnight Notes Collective, 99–100
modernization: capitalism and, 45, 49, 60, 62, 82, 84, 95–96, 114; inevitability of, 15, 28, 41, 114–19, 140, 142; opposition to, 3, 52–53; risks of, 34, 36, 56, 59, 61, 66, 74; theories of, 14, 29, 48, 50, 73, 83–84, 86, 113, 146; traditionalism and, 58, 61–62, 69–71, 74. *See also* capitalism; colonization; development; developmentalism; economies; heritage; imperialism; industrialization; technology
MONDIACULT, 55, 67
Mother and Child Protection Law (1937), 47
museumization, 57, 73, 118, 142

Nairobi Plan. *See* United Nations General Conference in Nairobi (1976)

National Endowment for the Arts, 152n10

National Eugenics Law (1940), 47

nationalism, 52–53, 90, 95, 140. *See also* colonization; globalism; governance; heritage; imperialism; media; statism

Nervous Conditions (Dangarembga), 134–36

New International Economic Order (NIEO), 59, 78, 84, 91, 96, 140

New World Information and Communications Order (NWICO), 59, 78, 91, 96, 140

The New Yorker, 44

Nigeria, 16, 72

Nobel Prize for Literature, 38, 44, 51, 59

nongovernmental organizations (NGOs), 101, 112, 127, 129, 133, 135–37, 146

Norwegian Agency for Development Cooperation (NORAD), 127

Norwich, 102

Offe, Claus, 149n1

Okai, Atukwei, 90

The Old Capital (Kawabata), 51

Oppenheimer Memorial Trust, 125, 137

Organization of American States, 25

Pakistan, 43

Palestine, 97, 143

Parsons, Talcott, 83

peace, 1, 5, 11, 15, 21, 26–27, 31, 37, 40, 108. *See also* globalism; policy making

Pellowski, Anne, 90

Penguin Books, 23

PEN International, 11–12, 23, 37, 41–42, 51, 142

People-to-People Initiative, 8

peripheral states. *See* developing world

Perry, Rachel, 57

piracy, 18–19, 81, 123–37, 142

Point Four Program, 27, 43

policy making: cultural, 15, 55–56, 68–70, 72–73, 85, 103, 114, 121–22, 130, 139, 147; global, 89, 106, 121; media and, 91, 93–94, 142; and reform, 1–3, 6–7, 12, 59, 78, 113

politics, 1, 7–12, 25, 39, 41, 69, 93, 120. *See also* governance; nationalism; statism

Politics (Aristotle), 25

Portuguese (language), 25

postcolonial states. *See* developing world

poverty: alleviation of, 30, 34, 59, 130; conditions of, 4, 31, 33, 56, 63; depictions of, 134–37, 146. *See also* Africa; capitalism; colonization; developing world; economies; employment; expropriation; extraction; imperialism; media; resources; unemployment

Prashad, Vijay, 35

Pritchett, V. S., 23

protest, 83, 140. *See also* radicalization; United States; Vietnam War

Protocol Regarding Developing Countries, 131

public-private partnerships, 17, 61, 81, 101, 111, 123, 130, 132

Publishers Weekly (magazine), 44

publishing industries, 5, 13, 24–25, 38, 78, 81, 87, 91–92, 102, 124. *See also* book industries; Britain; United States; *specific publishers*

Publishing in India (Altbach), 90

Pye, Lucian, 83

Qatar, 69

Qolorha, 115–17, 119–20

Quebec City, 102

Race and Culture (Leiris), 36

Race and History (Lévi-Strauss), 36

race and racism, 27, 29, 32–36, 134, 136, 140. *See also* biological determinism; Euro-centrism; Huxley, Julian; imperialism

Racial Myths (Comas), 36

radicalization, 4–9, 59, 61, 83, 140. *See also* policy making; protest
Rashomon (Kurosawa), 44
Rathgeber, Eva-Maria, 90
Read Locally!, 107
ReadPL, 105
Reproduction Rights Organization of Zimbabwe (ZIMCOPY), 18, 123–25, 129–30, 132
resources: distribution of, 36, 92, 96, 109, 132, 146; extraction of, 68, 125–27, 134–37, 139, 145. *See also* Africa; capitalism; developing world; economies; extraction; imperialism; marketization
Révolution du livre (Escarpit), 88
Reykjavik, 102
Rheams, Bryony, 124
Rhodes, Cecil, 134, 136
Rhodesia, 134
Rist, Gilbert, 14
Roads to Reading (Staiger), 90
Rockefeller, John D., III, 38
Rossellini, Roberto, 58
Rostow, Walter, 63, 83

Salih, Tayeb, 13, 69–73, 113, 142
Saunders, Frances Stonor, 8
Schlesinger Jr., Arthur, 11, 40
Schryer, Stephen, 9
Schultz, Theodore, 62
Schwartz, Henry, 39
science, 26–34, 67, 77, 95, 106, 144–45. *See also* development; knowledge; modernization; technology; universities
Seasons of Migration to the North (Salih), 69
Second World Black and African Festival of Arts and Culture (FESTAC), 16
Seidensticker, Edward, 38, 44, 49
Sembène, Ousmane, 55
Shakespeare, William, 25
Shanghai, 147
Shils, Edward, 83
Slaughter, Joseph, 94

Smith, John, 100
Smith, Keith, 90
Smith, Roger, 35
Smith Jr., Datus C., 90
Smithsonian Folklife Festival, 16
Snow Country (Kawabata), 11–12, 37–40, 44–51, 53, 69, 142
socialism, 31, 63, 94. *See also* capitalism; communism; USSR
socialization, 4, 7, 28, 32, 60, 68, 89
Society for International Cultural Relations, 37
Solana, Fernando, 67–68
South Africa, 114–17, 119–20
Soviet State Committee for Foreign Economic Relations, 81
Spanish (language), 25
Staiger, Ralph C., 90
standard of living, 26–27, 30, 32, 34, 56, 61, 63, 67, 86, 139, 141
"Statement on Race, Paris, July 1950," 34
"Statement on the Nature of Race and Race Difference, Paris, 1951," 35–36
statism: capitalism and, 78, 85–86, 103, 113, 126; culture and, 55–56, 74–75, 152n10; media and, 91, 94, 109; opposition to, 7, 82, 94. *See also* governance; policy making
Statistical Yearbook, 77
Staunton, Irene, 127–29
Stockholm Conference (1967), 131
Storia della colonna infame (Manzoni), 25
Strauss, Harold, 37, 39, 44
Structural Adjustment Programs (SAPs), 72, 99, 124, 127
Sudan, 70–72
suprahumanity, 27, 36, 44, 139. *See also* humanism; transhumanism
Sweden, 43
Swedish International Development Cooperation Agency (SIDA), 127
symbolism, 46–48, 53, 69–73, 114–19

technology: books as, 86, 105;

development of, 58, 64, 67, 77, 95, 106, 144; distribution of, 7, 26, 43, 63, 140; innovation and, 107, 112. *See also* development; industrialization; knowledge; science

textbooks, 95, 126–27. *See also* knowledge; publishing industries; universities

third world. *See* developing world

This September Sun (Rheam), 124

A Thousand Cranes (Kawabata), 51

Tokyo, 49, 88

totalitarianism, 10, 39–41. *See also* China; colonization; governance; imperialism; USSR

tourism: branding and, 1–2, 7, 119; cultural, 103–4, 142; as expropriation, 16, 18, 28, 52; industry, 17, 62, 101, 114–19, 147. *See also* culture; developing world; development; heritage; marketization; racism; wealth

trade, 43, 80, 86, 91, 97, 113, 124–25, 127, 140. *See also* Britain; capitalism; economies; Europe; United States; wealth

Traditional Market Agreement, 126

traditions: and branding, 16, 117; folk, 12, 46–47, 53, 142; preservation of, 41, 49–53, 113. *See also* culture; heritage; tourism

transhumanism, 26, 139

translation: accessibility and, 22, 38, 44, 102; of classic literature, 1, 10, 12, 21–26, 29, 33, 36–37, 88, 139; English, 12, 69. *See also* book industries; languages; publishing industries; *specific languages*

Travis, Trysh, 95

Truman, Harry, 27

Tzouvala, Konstantina, 14, 96, 140

unemployment, 16, 67, 128, 133, 143. *See also* capitalism; economies; employment; industrialization; labor; wealth

UNESCO Courier, 77, 84, 87

United International Bureaux for the Protection of Intellectual Property (BIRPI), 131

United Kingdom. *See* Britain

United Nations (UN), 13, 27, 63, 83, 133, 140

United Nations 1948 Declaration of Human Rights, 41

United Nations Development Program, 64

United Nations Fund for Economic Development, 43

United Nations General Conference in Nairobi (1976), 83–86

United Nations World Decade for Cultural Development, 55

United States: Army Languages Program, 38, 44; book industries in the, 89, 126, 130; and cities, 9, 61; as colonizer, 30, 35; and foreign policy, 27, 57, 83, 145; and governance, 8, 14, 52; and hegemony, 7, 9–14, 37–53, 66–67, 92, 139, 145, 149n1, 150n14; Information Service, 94; and UNESCO, 59, 64, 94, 97, 143. *See also* Britain; capitalism; economies; Europe; industrialization

United States Agency for International Development (USAID), 81–82, 87, 94

Universal Declaration of Human Rights, 57

universality, 4, 6, 40

universities, 7–9, 22, 25, 39, 102, 104, 127–28. *See also* Europe; knowledge; technology; wealth

unworlding, 4–5, 45, 73

urbanization, 40, 70, 72, 90, 99–102, 104, 125, 139, 152n10. *See also* agriculture; developing world; development; marketization; technology

USSR, 11, 14, 40, 43, 45, 89, 92, 94

Vietnam War, 52, 83
The Vital Center (Schlesinger Jr.), 40

Wallerstein, Immanuel, 96
War on Poverty (US), 9
Warwick Research Collective (WReC),
    3–4, 7
wealth: accumulation of, 32–33, 86, 101,
    110, 131; cultural, 7, 12, 16, 101;
    distribution of, 60, 66, 104, 125;
    extraction of, 43, 134; gap, 7, 100,
    137, 143; governance and, 34, 125;
    literature and, 1–2, 5, 128; power
    and, 4, 50, 102, 141; sources of,
    5, 109. *See also* capitalism; Euro-
    centrism; expropriation; extraction;
    labor; resources; tourism
Weaver Press, 127–29
We Europeans: A Survey of "Racial"
    Problems (Huxley & Haddon), 35
We Need New Names (Bulawayo), 18,
    124, 132–33, 135–36, 142, 146
West African Institute of Arts, 31
What Is a World? (Cheah), 3
"What is the History of Books?"
    (Darnton), 79

When People Play People (Mda), 120
Williams, Raymond, 8
Wirtén, Eva Hemmungs, 125, 129, 131
Woblink.com, 105
Woods, George, 62
World Bank, 59, 62–64, 66, 72, 99
World Book and Copyright Day, 11, 123,
    130
World Book Capitals, 102
World Conference on Cultural Policies
    (MONDIACULT), 55, 67
World Federation of Scientific Workers,
    23
World Heritage Sites, 26, 51, 70, 117,
    119
World Intellectual Property Organization
    (WIPO), 100

Xi Jinping, 144

Yale Review, 33
Yaoundé, 87
Yukiguni (Kawabata). *See Snow Country*
    (Kawabata)

Zimbabwe, 18, 123–24, 127–30, 132,
    134, 137
ZIMCOPY, 18, 123–25, 129–30, 132

Sophie Seita, *Provisional Avant-Gardes: Little Magazine Communities from Dada to Digital*

Guy Davidson, *Categorically Famous: Literary Celebrity and Sexual Liberation in 1960s America*

Joseph Jonghyun Jeon, *Vicious Circuits: Korea's IMF Cinema and the End of the American Century*

Lytle Shaw, *Narrowcast: Poetry and Audio Research*

Stephen Schryer, *Maximum Feasible Participation: American Literature and the War on Poverty*

Margaret Ronda, *Remainders: American Poetry at Nature's End*

Jasper Bernes, *The Work of Art in the Age of Deindustrialization*

Annie McClanahan, *Dead Pledges: Debt, Crisis, and Twenty-First-Century Culture*

Amy Hungerford, *Making Literature Now*

J. D. Connor, *The Studios after the Studios: Neoclassical Hollywood (1970–2010)*

Michael Trask, *Camp Sites: Sex, Politics, and Academic Style in Postwar America*

Loren Glass, *Counterculture Colophon: Grove Press, the* Evergreen Review, *and the Incorporation of the Avant-Garde*

Michael Szalay, *Hip Figures: A Literary History of the Democratic Party*

Jared Gardner, *Projections: Comics and the History of Twenty-First-Century Storytelling*

Jerome Christensen, *America's Corporate Art: The Studio Authorship of Hollywood Motion Pictures*

Made in the USA
Columbia, SC
30 December 2020